Tapestry
of
Healing

Where
Reiki and Medicine Intertwine

Jeri Mills, M.D.

White Sage Press

The material contained in this book is not intended as medical advice. If you have a medical illness, consult a qualified physician.

Cover photo by Jeri Mills
Cover design by Ghost River Images

Published by White Sage Press, P.O. Box 1022 , Green Valley, Arizona 85622.

http://www.TapestryOfHealing.com

Printed in the United States of America

Library of Congress Control Number 2001094791

ISBN 0-9713350-0-1

*For my father who brought the
gift of storytelling into my life*

Contents

Acknowledgements

I wish to thank my dear friends Moneen and Walt Lang, whose belief in me and in my ability to complete this project have seen me through the most difficult moments.

I also wish to thank Moneen Lang, Walt Lang, Jan Lorimer, Pat Felix, Samuel Correnti and Marsha Seng for the support, encouragement and advice that have helped this book to attain its final form.

Special gratitude to Mike and Tama White who helped to rekindle the joy and excitement that have been the driving force behind the creation of this book.

Introduction

Contemporary society has turned healing into medicine and medicine into a sophisticated job of plumbing. *Tapestry of Healing* describes the evolution of a marriage of Western medicine and Reiki that transforms the practice of medicine back into healing.

Reiki is an ancient hands-on healing art that brings harmony to the body, mind, and spirit. Historically, the teaching of Reiki has been a strictly verbal tradition. Over the years I have discovered, to my dismay, that many of my own students as well as acquaintances who have been the students of other Reiki Masters are often hesitant to use their healing abilities because they have forgotten much of the information presented in their classes. It is with these people in mind that I decided to include not only the story of my experiences, but a basic course in energy medicine and Reiki in this book. I have attempted to share the pearls and pitfalls that I encountered on my personal journey into energy medicine.

The material in this book has been presented in a way that should be easily understood by those with no previous knowledge of Eastern healing arts. My goal is to inform the uninitiated while still providing some new insights for the experienced healer.

I believe that the integration of Western medicine with energy medicine helps us achieve a level of health and healing that is infinitely greater than either school can achieve on its own. It is my sincere hope that sharing my experiences will encourage others to open themselves to the possibility of accepting this medical marriage. I invite you to help me weave this Tapestry of Healing.

Prologue

It was just past 1 A.M. when I rolled out of bed in the doctors' on-call room and headed towards labor wing. As I walked through the door to the labor and delivery triage room, the familiar smell of alcohol and iodine filled my nostrils. The room vibrated with the low drumming of half a dozen fetal cardiac monitors, a soothing melody for those of us who worked on labor and delivery. The slightest alteration of any of those rhythms would alert us and send everyone running to handle the emergency.

I went to the desk where the nurse on duty handed me a chart and gave me a brief history of the patient who had just arrived.

As I walked down the narrow aisle separating the two rows of gurneys that lined the walls of the room, I heard an occasional voice coming from behind the curtains that shielded occupied beds. Most patients were there to determine if they were in labor. Others were pregnant, ill, and waiting for lab tests to come back. Some anxious women came to check on the well-being of a fetus who had been less active than usual that evening.

I opened the curtain to the dimly lit six-by-nine foot cubicle where my patient rested on a gurney. Long, narrow feet moved restlessly. Slender fingers convulsively gripped the edge of the blanket that covered an enormous belly. Two gray plastic cords snaked out from under the blanket connecting the sensors that were belted over my patient's abdomen to the fetal monitor in the back corner of the cubicle near her right shoulder.

Enormous brown eyes stared at me from a pale face. A tentative smile crossed her lips only to be replaced by a grimace as the next contraction began.

The woman's back arched and she reached frantically for the arm of the small, round, gray-haired woman who stood at her left side. The older woman gently rubbed the pregnant woman's shoulder as she murmured soft, reassuring sounds.

When the contraction subsided, I introduced myself. The pregnant woman's hand trembled slightly when she reached out to shake mine.

"This is my mother," she told me in an unsteady voice. "She had to come with me tonight because my husband is out of town."

Her voice broke and a small sob escaped her lips. She took a deep breath and continued.

"This is my fourth baby. I should be used to it by now, but this labor is much worse than all the other ones. He seems to be in such a hurry, this little one."

She stopped speaking and reached out for her mother's hand as the next contraction began. As soon as it was over, I examined my patient. Though her labor had started less than two hours earlier, she was already eight centimeters dilated. Two more centimeters and her baby would be ready to enter this world.

I alerted the nursing staff and we quickly rolled her down the hall to a nearby birthing room. We had just gotten her settled in the room when she began writhing in the bed.

I said, "There's no time for an epidural, your baby is coming too fast, but I can give you an injection of pain medicine."

"No," she gasped. "I had all my other babies naturally. I won't take drugs for this Aieeeee..."

Unable to use any of the tools Western medicine had to offer to relieve my patient's discomfort, there was still one thing I could do to help her.

After obtaining her permission, I laid my hands lightly on her swollen abdomen. The healing energy immediately began to flow through my palms. My patient gave a long sigh and her shoulders seemed to melt into the pillows. Her fingers slowly released the balled-up edge of the blanket. Looking at me through heavy lidded eyes, she mumbled, "Oh, I'm so relaxed..."

After a few minutes, her eyes closed. The energy continued to flow from my hands, and she appeared to sleep through the next several contractions.

Reassured that my patient was comfortable, I left her side and walked across the room to her mother. As we chatted softly about the various applications of the ancient hands-on healing art, I asked the woman if she would like to see how it felt. At her nod, I placed my hands at her temples and relieved the headache she had developed over the last hours.

Awakened by an intense pain, my patient looked at me and demanded, "I want you back here with me right now!"

I returned to her bedside and placed one hand near the top of her uterus and the other above her pelvis. There I remained, a living epidural, until she delivered her son a half hour later.

How did this American-trained obstetrician gynecologist come to combine Western medicine with ancient Buddhist healing techniques while practicing in a hospital in Tucson, Arizona? Looking back, it amazes even me to recall the subtle twists of fate that shaped the healer I was to become.

PART ONE

My Journey

The first peace, which is the most important,
is that which comes within the souls of people when they
realize their relationship, their oneness, with the universe
and all its powers, and when they realize that at the center
of the universe dwells the Great Spirit, and that this
center is really everywhere, it is within each of us.

~Black Elk

CHAPTER ONE

How It All Began

My early years were divided between winters spent in Cleveland, Ohio, and the rest of the year traveling with my father's circus.

While with the circus, if I wasn't reading a book, I was with the animals. Most afternoons, I could be found in the company of a big, black horse named Hawk. He stood patiently by while I described my mad crush on the handsome young lion trainer. His giant head gently rubbed my shoulder when I tearfully reported that my mother had, yet again, refused to let me go on an outing with the other children. He was my best friend.

Starting at age seven, I was sent to live with my mother's sister for several months at the beginning and end of each school year. My parents believed they were doing what was best for me, making sure I didn't miss any school while they were traveling with the circus.

To a homesick little girl, the endless months in the big, lonely house far from parents and across town from school and friends, were sheer torture. Books became my closest companions. Missing other children and my beloved animals from the circus, I repeatedly brought home orphaned baby birds and bunnies and tried to nurse them back to health.

For years I resented not only the time I was forced to live with my relatives, but also school in general. That all changed when I was in the fifth grade. Sitting at my desk one day feeling angry and sorry for myself, I suddenly realized that the resentment wasn't going to change anything.

I decided it was time to find a reason to want to be where I was. An image flashed into my mind of myself as an adult. I was a physician. I was busy, happy, and surrounded by people who needed me. In that instant, I decided to become a doctor when I grew up. School was suddenly transformed from a punishment into the most important place in my life. Education was going to get me where I was determined to go. From that day on, whenever I was sad or lonely, I closed my eyes and imagined myself in a future time where an adult Jeri cared for people just as the child took care of injured animals.

At fifteen, the thought of more lonely years with my relatives became unbearable. I begged to be allowed to go to boarding school. Unlike the image of strict, regimented boarding schools conjured up by a Dickens novel, for me going away to school meant finally living with people my own age, having friends, and being part of a community. The prospect was intoxicating. I chose a school in Sedona, Arizona, because I would be able to bring my horse along with me.

Prior to that time, nothing in my background had even hinted at the possibility of a spiritual universe.

I considered myself to be a staunch atheist. That was all to change in Sedona.

My spiritual awakening didn't arrive like a bolt of lightning in the middle of the wilderness, but it did arrive. The desert held a special magic for me. The land pulsated with life. For the first time, I felt a strong emotional bond with the earth. The ancient spirits of the desert warmed my heart as they touched my soul. As I became conscious of the presence of those spirits around me, I began to believe there was more to humanity than mere flesh and blood. I started to search for answers.

The second event that year that was to play a large role in shaping my future was more prosaic but certainly no less significant to the final outcome. My boyfriend introduced me to science fiction and fantasy novels. In my favorite books, the scientific and the mystical intertwined. People traveled in spaceships and on the backs of telepathic dragons. Characters had psychic abilities. A surgeon was as likely to cut with a crystal as a scalpel. People performed healings with their minds. Visions of those wonderful worlds filled my dreams when the limitations of contemporary life left me feeling helpless and frustrated.

After spending my sophomore year in Sedona, I dropped out of high school. Later that year, I was able to talk my way into college. What must have been a compelling essay got me admitted on probation. Grades that kept me on the dean's honor list allowed me to stay there without restrictions. I still had a driving ambition to go to medical school.

During my junior year in college I had two pets, a Malamute dog and a pure-bred wolf that I had hand raised from the time he was seven days old. One evening while chatting with a friend I said, "You know, David, I don't know how I'll ever manage medical school and internship. I can't imagine being away from these dogs all night."

"Well, then, why don't you become a veterinarian instead?" he suggested. "You won't have to be an intern and stay in the hospital over night."

"What a great idea!" I innocently replied. Little did I know that both veterinarians and physicians spend many nights away from home throughout their entire careers.

It might have ended there, just an interesting idea, but a few days later I went to discuss the idea with the pre-med advisor at my college. The man was the only professor in the biology department whom I actively disliked. When I told him I was thinking about going to vet school, he started laughing at me.

"I tried to get into vet school myself and was never accepted," he said. "YOU certainly don't stand a chance of getting in."

Never one to ignore a challenge, I applied to veterinary school and was accepted. The course of my life changed because of a moment of temper.

I liked veterinary medicine well enough, but by the end of the first school year, I realized that my childhood dream to be a physician was as strong as ever. I knew I would eventually go back to school to become a medical doctor.

In the mean time, I graduated from vet school and got a job working in a small animal emergency clinic. I loved the animals. I came to adore dealing with emergencies, especially the emergency surgeries I frequently performed. In an effort to explain just how exciting it was to perform major surgery, I once told a friend that if I ever had to choose between operating on a dog with a gastric torsion or going on a date with Robert Redford, I would choose to do the operation.

After three years as a veterinarian, I started medical school. I loved medicine with an all-consuming passion. As a new physician, I believed there was no god more powerful than the god of Almighty Science, but the more I learned, the more aware I became of the limitations of modern medicine. It was depressing to realize just how much we could *not* do. Western medicine can prevent plagues and provide miraculous cures for the victims of trauma and acute illness. In spite of this, Western medicine has little to offer the people afflicted by many chronic disorders. I sensed there had to be something more.

Through the years, my great escape from the stress and exhaustion of practicing medicine continued to be science fiction and fantasy novels. I never imagined that the magic and the abilities I read about would actually become a part of my reality in this lifetime. And then I moved to Tucson, Arizona.

*Life confronts us with two doors.One is the
apparently easy choice: To go with the flow, to
pursue our desires, to seek security and comfort.
The other offers risk and uncertainty. It is the inner
search for our truth.*
~Journal Notes:The Quiet Entity
by Rod MacIver

CHAPTER TWO

Tucson:
Learning to Channel Energy

In 1991, my first job after residency training was with an obstetrics and gynecology practice in east Tennessee. When I arrived there, I bought a small house on top of a big hill. The first time we visited the house, I turned to the realtor and said, "Well, this place may get blown away by a tornado, but I'll never have to worry about floods up here." Famous last words.

The movers were carrying the last of my belongings into the house when water started pouring through the dining room ceiling. It streamed from the light fixture like a fountain, creating a lake on my new carpet. That was only the first of five floods to occur during my first six months in the house. Pipes burst, water heaters overflowed, drain pipes were left disconnected, the dishwasher turned on with its door open. The Stanley Steemer truck spent so much time in my driveway that my neighbor thought I was having an affair with the carpet cleaning man.

The last straw came when I returned from my first weekend trip. As the garage door began to rise,

I saw a paper taped to the bottom of the door, flapping in the breeze. The note said, "There was water in the house when I came to feed your cats. Your neighbor came over and turned it off."

With great trepidation, I unlocked the door, removed my shoes, and walked into the living room on the middle level of my three-story home. Water squished between my toes as I moved across the soggy pink carpet. I walked downstairs to the ground level and was horrified by the scene that greeted me. A musty smell assailed my nostrils. The wet plaster of the ceiling sagged under the weight of a pool of trapped water. A crack dripped dirty water onto the puddle in the center of the family room. The wood paneling, heavy with water, bowed away from the walls. With a shaky hand I reached for the phone and, yet again, called Stanley Steemer to begin the job of flood repairs.

I was now convinced that something did not want me to stay in that house. I didn't know where I was supposed to go, but I knew I'd better make some changes before things got even worse. I had visions of a roof crashing in on my head as I slept.

Later that day, when the tears had dried and the carpets were drying, I stood in the back yard looking up at the sky and said, "I guess Spirit is telling me to move to the desert." That must have been the answer because there were no more floods.

A few months later, I vacationed in Tucson, Arizona. After one horseback ride in the Catalina Mountains, I was in love. The stark beauty of the desert touched me in a way the green prettiness of

Tennessee had never matched. Delicate flowers buried between the spiny branches of cactus seemed to promise something fine and precious in that harsh wilderness. As I rode past a stand of ancient sahuaros, I could feel the pull of past civilizations who had lived on this land. It was as though their spirits had come back to live in the giant cactus, to guard the land that had been their home.

In all my travels I had never before encountered such a mystical place. I was overwhelmed by a feeling of belonging.

Though I returned to Tennessee, a part of me remained in Arizona. The desert called to me like a lover, and I knew I must return.

Having no idea where I would live or where I would work, I quit my job the following spring and moved to Tucson.

There were moments of doubt and, occasionally, abject terror as I packed up my household and drove across the country with two dogs and two cats as my only companions. It didn't take long to be reassured that I had made the right decision.

Since I was a child, I have always sketched in the margins of class notes, study guides, or any other paper that came into my hands. The same portrait of a face with an oddly shaped head has appeared on my papers over and over again throughout the years. Shortly after arriving in Tucson, I sat in my back yard one evening to watch the sunset. Gazing across the skyline, I discovered, to my utter amazement, that the face I had been drawing all my life was not a face at all. I had been drawing a silhouette of the section of the Catalina Mountains directly north of my house! This place had been calling to me since I was a child! I knew with complete and utter certainty that I was in exactly the place I was supposed to be. For the first time in my life, I had found home.

My first summer in Arizona was spent on a journey of self-discovery. I looked toward the etheric and the spiritual. The mountains and the desert embraced me in their magic spell. The ancient spirits of the sahuaros seemed to whisper my name as they welcomed me into their land.

After learning how to meditate, doors into the world of alternative healing began to open before me of their own accord. I was introduced to the principles of shamanic healing in a wonderful book called *Soul Retrieval* by Sandy Ingerman. Shamanic journeys allowed me to retrieve lost parts of myself, to become whole. The journey into shamanic traditions led me to explore other Native American healing practices. Some day, all of these modalities and more would come together to shape the healer I was to become.

I attended a creativity workshop at Pima College. The instructor, Diane Ealy, was an elfin woman with a ready smile, a sharp wit, and a Ph.D. in psychology. During the workshop she mentioned that she was able to channel energy for healing. This was my first encounter with a real person who claimed to be able to do what I had been dreaming about my whole life!

At a lunch meeting a few weeks later, I asked Diane about the energy work. She told me she could channel healing energy from the earth into her body and out through the palms of her hands. My heart lit up. I asked if anyone could learn how to do this energy channeling. She said yes. When I asked if she would teach me she agreed. We never managed to find the time to get together for the lessons, but the seeds were planted.

Within a few months, I started working in the obstetrics and gynecology department of a large, multispecialty medical practice.

Prior to entering the office or hospital each morning, I always allowed myself a few minutes to sit in the car and go through a series of meditation exercises. In my favorite meditation, I imagined myself to be inhaling healing energy from the earth through the soles of my feet and exhaling it out the top of my head. I breathed universal energy in through the top of my head and exhaled it out my feet into the earth. These sessions always made me feel calm and centered.

One day on call, I admitted a fifteen-year-old Hispanic girl in active labor. She spoke no English, and I speak little Spanish. She had no prenatal education.

When I entered her hospital room, she was thrashing in the bed and tears streaked her face. She cowered in the corner of the bed, her arms wrapped protectively around her body. As the next contraction hit, she let out a piercing wail. Her baby's father, a boy who didn't look a day over thirteen, awkwardly patted her back with a tremulous hand. His jaw clenched and he looked as though he might burst into tears himself at any minute.

Speaking softly to the girl, I took her hand. With words and gestures, I got her to focus her attention on me and encouraged her to join me in taking slow, deep breaths. As she began to concentrate on her breathing, the tears stopped and the death grip she had on my hand started to relax.

We continued to hold hands and take slow deep breaths together. After a few minutes, her panic completely disappeared and she was perfectly still. I suddenly realized I had been doing the energy channeling meditation. This time, however, the energy I inhaled was entering my heart, moving down my arm, and then traveling from the palm of my hand into her hand. My patient was now able to relax and sit still long enough to receive an epidural. After the epidural, she fell asleep for the first time in twenty-four hours. She woke after a few hours, still calm and comfortable, and delivered her baby into a peaceful, reassuring environment.

At home that evening, anxious to share the experience, I phoned Diane. After relating the story of the young girl, I told her I thought I had been channeling energy. She said, "Of course you have." After we talked a little more about hands-on healing, she encouraged me to continue the practice now that I had discovered how to channel energy.

Having always worked in large, group practices, I often did not meet my patients prior to taking care of them in labor. In order to develop a better rapport with those patients, I always spent as much time as possible in the labor room getting to know my patient and her family before the time of delivery.

Being very physical by nature, I would usually hold a patient's hand or rest a hand on her shoulder while helping her breathe through contractions. I often supported her in my arms when she received an epidural. The fact that I was always in the room with my patients and frequently in physical contact with them, made it an easy, natural transition to do energy work.

After my conversation with Diane, whenever a patient was upset or in pain, I would touch her and channel energy for her. My patients always felt better. It was incredible to be able to relieve their distress with the touch of my hands, but there was a problem. Sometimes after those sessions, I felt wonderful. At other times, I went home feeling completely drained. As I lay on the bed those evenings, it felt like my life force was somewhere under the bed, my spirit too weak to stay inside my body.

I called Diane to see if she could shed some light on the situation. She explained that sometimes I was channeling energy from the earth or the universe but at other times I was giving away my own energy.

She finally decided to teach the class we had discussed so many months earlier.

With Diane's guidance, I achieved the focus necessary to consistently draw energy from the earth or universe into my heart and then to channel it out of my hands. No longer would I be at risk of giving my own life force away. Diane also taught several shielding techniques that would prevent me from picking up other people's pain or negative emotions.

In that one-day workshop, I also met another healer who was to play an important part in my own development as a healer. He would introduce me to the use of crystals in healing work, and our relationship would lead me to a deeper understanding of both the scope and the ethics of distance healing.

Diane ended the workshop with a lengthy discussion about the ethics of hands-on healing work. As with any other form of treatment, we felt the subject's consent should be obtained before channeling energy. It was decided that permission could be requested either verbally or psychically.

Not yet prepared to openly discuss the energy work in the hospital, I silently asked permission to channel energy for my patient while holding her hand. If she continued to hold onto my hand, I took that as a sign she was willing for the process to take place. If she let go, I backed off immediately. Most of them held onto me like I was a lifeline.

While channeling energy for my patient, I often led her through a guided meditation. My patients seemed to appreciate and benefit immensely from the energy work. In spite of this, I remained hesitant to openly discuss the process on labor wing.

I occasionally ran energy on the abdomens of post-op patients when we were alone in their hospital room. At those times, I did the work with their verbal permission. I asked if they would allow me to run a little energy over them to try to make them feel better. Being in Tucson, Arizona, most people had heard of such things. To my amazement, regardless of religious or ethnic background, no one ever refused. As I channeled energy for them, they frequently delighted me with stories of grandmothers with the healing touch and other previous healing experiences.

At first I turned to energy work only as a last resort, when traditional therapies were unable to help my patient. One such patient was a woman on whom I had performed a Caesarian section two days earlier. Her intestinal function still had not returned to normal. Drugs and standard medical procedures had done little to relieve her sharp abdominal pain. I offered to "try this energy technique that I had recently learned"; she agreed.

After running energy over her abdomen for about fifteen minutes, her pain was gone. My patient turned to me with an angry expression on her face and snapped, "Why didn't you do this for me two days ago?"

The next woman I visited during rounds that morning was a nurse from the emergency department at the practice where I worked. My partner, Jack, had performed a hysterectomy on her a day or two earlier. She, too, was having a lot of abdominal pain. With newfound confidence, I immediately offered to channel healing energy for this woman. Her pain quickly subsided.

Suspecting he didn't believe in this sort of thing, I asked her not to discuss the energy channeling with Jack. Though I didn't tell the patient, I was more than a little afraid my partners might object to my use of alternative healing methods. I was still not ready for office confrontations.

She came to the office some weeks later to thank me for the energy treatment, and asked if I thought she could learn to do it herself. The woman also informed me that she had told Jack all about the energy treatment I gave her in the hospital. She wanted him to know just how helpful it was. So much for secrets.

The most memorable experience during my early days of channeling energy was with an obstetric patient named Amy.

Amy's pregnancy had been plagued by one complication after another ever since its conception. At twenty-five weeks gestation, she was admitted to the hospital with severe pre-eclampsia. (*A full-term pregnancy lasts forty weeks.*)

Pre-eclampsia is a condition that causes dangerously high blood pressure. The patient may also experience damage to the liver and kidneys. She is at risk of developing seizures that can lead to permanent brain damage from strokes. The symptoms of pre-eclampsia generally resolve when the baby is delivered.

We hoped medications would prevent Amy from having seizures. Our goal was to keep her stabilized until her pregnancy was far enough along for her baby to have a reasonable chance of survival and a good quality of life after he was delivered.

Amy had been in the hospital about ten days when she began to show signs of heart failure. When I went into her room to check on her, the back of the bed was raised into a semi-sitting position and pillows were piled behind her back and under her knees. The color had drained from her cheeks until she was as pale as the sheets. Amy shifted restlessly in the bed trying to find a comfortable position. She pressed both hands into the top of her uterus in an attempt to push away the pain beneath her breast bone that was causing her to have difficulty breathing. Her respirations were short and shallow, like a runner on the last leg of a marathon. She was trying valiantly to keep going. Just a little farther.

"She's been like this for hours," the nurse told me. "She hasn't been able to sleep at all in the last two days."

"Amy," I began, "sometimes I'm able to talk people to sleep. Would you like me to try to do that with you?"

"Sure," she replied.

After silently asking permission to channel energy for Amy, I took her hand. The energy began to flow through my palm as I led her through a guided meditation.

"Close your eyes. Take slow, deep breaths. Now imagine that you are on a beach. The sun is shining on you. The sand is warm and soft. Your body is comfortable and relaxed. Your son is a strong, healthy little boy now. You see him off in the distance building sand castles with his daddy. Reassured that he is well and safe, you close your eyes and drift off into a peaceful sleep."

She clung to my energy hand like a drowning man hangs onto a life raft. After a few minutes, her breathing became slow and regular and she was fast asleep.

Even in sleep, she held on to my hand and continued to receive energy for quite a while. When she finally released my hand, I left the room. The nurse continued to monitor her, and I went to a nearby nurses' station to do some charting.

About two hours later, Amy's nurse came to the nurses' station looking quite stunned. She said, "The darndest thing just happened. Amy woke up a few minutes ago, and she's bouncing all over the room talking about how wonderful she feels! A few hours ago she could just barely walk the eight feet from her bed to the bathroom."

The next day, Amy was delivered by Caeserian section. Her son spent over ten months in the intensive care nursery, but ultimately did fairly well.

She and I never discussed the energy work I had done the night before her baby was born, but Amy must have known.

Whenever I ran into Amy leaving the nursery, which was just next to labor wing, we'd stop to chat. On three or four occasions she was with a friend or relative I had not met yet. She always introduced me to them by saying, "This is Dr. Mills. She's the one who saved my life the night before Matthew was born."

The next door into the world of energy medicine opened before me when I was in the office seeing patients. A woman I had never seen before came to me for a gynecology appointment.

She said, "Your name seemed to light up when I opened my provider manual. I prefer women doctors, but with a name like Jeri, I didn't know you were female when I made the appointment. I just knew you were the one I was supposed to see."

We were still chatting when I noticed the pendant that hung from a chain around her neck. It was inscribed with some sort of symbols.

"That looks very powerful," I said.

She got this secret little smile and replied, "I do hands-on healing."

The dam opened. I proceeded to tell this woman, this patient whom I had met only moments earlier, about Amy and all my other experiences channeling energy in the hospital.

She smiled again and said, "What I do will make what you do work better."

She was a Reiki Master. Until that moment, I had never even heard of Reiki. The woman was Theresa who was to become my teacher. The time we were to spend together would forever change my life. She was right, what she taught me did make what I already did work much better.

*And the time came when the risk it took to
remain tight inside the bud
Was more painful than the risk it took
to blossom...*
~Anais Nin

CHAPTER THREE

Coming Out of the Closet

For months after learning Reiki, I didn't discuss it openly in the hospital. After silently asking permission, I gave my patients partial treatments, with one hand casually placed on their head or abdomen. This was all about to change.

The day began like any other day on call. I arrived on labor wing shortly before 8A.M. After changing from street clothes into the teal scrubs provided by the hospital, I pulled on the color-coordinated flannel shirt I always wore instead of a traditional white lab coat. I draped my stethoscope around my neck, stuck a pen in my pocket, and went to find my partner who had been on call the previous night. We discussed the medical histories of the hospitalized patients who would be in my care for the next twenty-four hour shift; then I went to meet them.

First, I went to see sixteen-year-old Maria who had been laboring all night with her first baby, contracting every two to three minutes since her admission at 2A.M. When I opened her door, Maria shifted restlessly in the bed. Her hands grasped the plastic IV tubing and fetal monitor cords that restricted her movement. Her eyes held the look of a wolf caught in a leg-hold trap. A contraction hit and her arms reached frantically for her mother who sat beside her. Fresh tears streamed down Maria's face as her fingers dug into the older woman's shoulders.

Maria's aunt stood at the bedside. The aunt's fingers dug convulsively into the damp wash cloth she carried. As she stood by, unable to offer any assistance, a tear escaped the corner of her eye.

Maria's mother spoke softly as she gently pushed back the waves of long, black hair and wiped her daughter's brow with a soft cloth. No sooner had the girl started to relax than another contraction hit. Overwhelmed, her body arched in a spasm of pain.

When I was able to examine Maria, I discovered, to my dismay, that her cervix was no more dilated than it had been six hours earlier. Her baby was enormous. His head floated in her abdomen with little promise of entering her pelvis. I feared my young patient would have to be delivered by Caesarian section.

One of two situations can lead to the type of labor Maria was experiencing. Either the contractions are not strong enough to deliver the baby or the baby is simply too big to fit through the mother's pelvis. The usual management is to try to control the patient's pain and to use a drug called pitocin in an attempt to make the contractions stronger and more frequent so that a vaginal delivery might be possible.

After discussing the situation with Maria and her family, I recommended that we start pitocin. I also offered her an epidural for pain control. Despite her exhaustion and the fact that her labor had not progressed during the night, Maria was still determined to have natural childbirth. She refused all medical intervention.

My hands were tied. She wouldn't let me try to help her with any of the tools Western medicine had to offer. Without some assistance, I doubted she would be able to deliver her baby vaginally. I decided it was time for me to come out of the closet about energy medicine. Taking a deep breath, I cast aside my fears of what public knowledge of my use of energy medicine might mean to my career, and turned to face Maria.

"I recently learned this thing called Reiki," I told her. "It's an ancient hands-on healing art which allows me to channel healing energy from the universe through my hands into you. I'd be happy to give you a treatment if you like. I believe it might help to relieve your pain, but the only thing I can guarantee is that it will cause no harm."

A small, hopeful smile crossed her lips. She said, "Oh yes. When I was a little girl, my *Abuelita* could take away the pain with her hands too." Maria's family seemed relieved by my suggestion, they didn't find it the least bit odd. As Spirit would have it, the nurse assigned to my patient that morning was a friend of mine who was already aware of the fact that I was a Reiki practitioner. This nurse was later to become one of my Reiki students.

A shiver of excitement ran down my spine. For the first time, I was about to give someone a full Reiki treatment in the hospital!

Maria lay down and I moved behind the head of the bed and lifted my hands to her temples. My hands tingled as the Reiki energy poured through my palms like a warm, rich fluid. After only a few minutes, her body relaxed into the bed and the haunted expression left her eyes. She began to breathe more slowly as she regained her self-control. Thirty minutes later, when I left the room to check on another patient, Maria reclined comfortably against a pile of pillows. Her mother held her left hand, her aunt held her right. Native American flute music played softly in the background and my young patient breathed through her contractions with the serenity of a Madonna.

Two hours later, she was fully dilated. After only forty-five minutes of pushing, *(first babies usually take about two hours of pushing)*, accompanied by soft music and loving encouragement, without even requiring an episiotomy, Maria delivered her ten pound twelve ounce son.

The experience was a turning point in my life. I realized Reiki was too valuable to be kept secret any longer. From that day forward, I offered a Reiki treatment to every labor patient in my care. With only one exception, they all accepted.

I saw magic happen. My C-section rate went down to less than one per month. My patients no longer had long, protracted labors. Women who previously had Caeserian sections for seven pound babies were having nine and ten pound babies vaginally.

Even though women in early labor experience a lot of pain, we are hesitant to offer medication because it may stop labor if given too soon. I could give Reiki treatments in early labor with no ill affect. My patients were much more relaxed and comfortable. Many of them slept until they were far enough along to receive pain medicine. Some slept until it was time to push. Reiki alone controlled the pain for the entire labor. Babies came out calm but vigorous with strong vital signs.

It was incredible. This was one of the most joyful times in my life. I had achieved the dream of anyone who dedicates her life to medicine. I could make people feel better with a touch of my hand.

Staying with your beauty, your truth, your integrity,
is difficult, but out of these things comes meaning,
and meaning is all-transcendent.
~Journal Notes: The Quiet Entity
by Rod MacIver

CHAPTER FOUR

Miracle

Another thread was woven into the tapestry of healing when I was, as usual, on labor wing. One of my partners sent in a patient who needed to be delivered emergently. An ultrasound exam earlier that day showed almost no amniotic fluid left around the baby. Without amniotic fluid there was a risk that the baby would roll over, crush her umbilical cord, and die in utero. Our plan was to keep the woman on continuous fetal monitoring and to give her a medication to induce her labor.

I had never met this woman prior to her arrival at the hospital that evening, so she had no special expectations or pre-conceived notions about me or the energy work I did.

I admitted her and explained what we wanted to do. The woman was started on a pitocin drip and given something to help her sleep. She awoke at about 5A.M. in active labor. She moved restlessly about the bed, tensing up and panting through each contraction.

"Please," she gasped, "can't I have something for the pain?"

I couldn't offer her an epidural because she suffered from a condition that caused her to have a very low platelet count. Her platelet count was so low that inserting an epidural would risk causing a hemorrhage into her spinal cord. I was hesitant to give her very much intravenous pain medicine because she was only four centimeters dilated and there was a risk of stopping her labor with drugs. I decided to give her five milligrams of Nubain, a dose that would help her to relax between contractions, but, in all honesty, would probably not do a lot to relieve the pain.

When she had received her medication, I offered her a Reiki treatment which she accepted.

Stepping behind the head of the bed to begin her treatment, I was unable to see the fetal monitor. The labor nurse continued to watch it closely.

With my hands at her temples, the Reiki began to flow. While healing energy moved through her body, I began to lead her through a guided meditation. Within a few minutes, she was fast asleep.

"Oh shoot," I thought. "I must have given this woman too much Nubain and stopped her labor."

I asked the nurse if the woman's contractions had stopped.

She said, "No, they're still every two minutes."

I continued my treatment.

Even though she was sleeping, I continued speaking to my patient. "Imagine the baby is inside a long, dark tunnel. The walls of the tunnel are slowly melting away to make room as the baby glides towards a light at the opening. While you continue to watch your baby gliding down the tunnel, I want you to send reassuring thoughts to your little one. Picture yourself holding the baby in your arms and send that picture to the baby. Tell her how much you love her and how anxious you are to see her and to hold her. Tell her to come out and meet her mommy."

About twenty minutes later, as I reached the patient's feet with my treatment, she began to breathe heavily with each contraction. The thought crossed my mind that she might be ready to push. My logical mind reminded me that no woman sleeps through a twenty-minute labor with only five milligrams of Nubain for pain relief. (*Short labors are generally very intense.*)

With the next contraction, she breathed hard again. Ignoring my logical self, I asked, "Do you think you might be ready to push?"

The nurse's head whipped around. Mouth wide open, she stared at me like she thought I had lost my mind.

In a soft, sleepy voice, my patient said, "Yes, I might."

Getting ready to check her, I moved the blankets aside. The baby's head was sitting on the woman's perineum, a four-inch circle of dark curly hair already protruding.

"Your baby is right here, ready to be born," I said. "Do you think you could wait for just a minute so we can get some instruments ready?"

"Oh sure," she answered in a soft, unconcerned voice.

The nurse ripped open an emergency delivery pack as I quickly donned gown and sterile gloves. With only two pushes, my patient delivered her little daughter. After clamping and cutting the cord, I placed the baby on her mother's abdomen. To my utter amazement, the baby began to squirm and appeared to crawl up to her mother's chest!

The nurse turned to me with a funny expression on her face and said, "Well, you did tell her to come out and meet her mother!"

Later that morning, I happily related this new Reiki story to the staff at my office. Little did I know, the real miracle was yet to come.

The following day, in the hospital elevator, I encountered a labor wing nurse coming off the night shift. She had been nowhere near the hospital when I had my wonderful Reiki delivery the previous morning.

She said to me, "Dr. Mills, the whole labor wing is talking about what you did yesterday. CAN YOU TEACH US?"

CHAPTER FIVE
Surgery

Once I began using Reiki openly on labor wing, I started offering Reiki treatments to all my surgery patients as well. Before an operation, I obtained permission from my patient to give her a Reiki treatment after surgery.

I then gave her a complete Reiki treatment when she was in the recovery room. After balancing her energy system, I reconnected the energy lines that had been severed at the same time knives had cut through my patient's physical body.

It was interesting to observe the reactions of nurses and anesthesiologists as I stood in the big, open recovery room, surrounded by patients on ventilators, attached to blinking cardiac monitors, and proceeded to perform a hands-on healing. Some people asked what I was doing and I quietly explained the process to them. Others carefully avoided making eye contact with me. Some even took a path around the far side of the room to avoid contact with me as they went about their duties.

Patients who received post-operative Reiki treatments seemed to require less pain medicine after surgery. Even I was surprised with the dramatic results experienced by one young woman on whom I had performed an abdominal hysterectomy.

Jane, an athletic woman in her early thirties, had a very easy post-operative course. She was released from the hospital about thirty-six hours after surgery. After giving her a prescription for pain medicine, I explained the usual post-op precaution and advised her to avoid strenuous exercise and heavy lifting for six weeks.

A week after the operation, I saw her in the office to remove her sutures. "I feel great," she informed me. "I only took one pain pill the afternoon I arrived home from the hospital. After that, I never needed to take anything stronger than Tylenol for pain relief."

Before she left the office, I reminded her, "Now, no matter how well you feel, remember you just had major surgery. Walking is good for you but it takes six weeks for the incision to become strong, so take it easy. Don't do any heavy lifting or anything to strain your abdominal muscles. Take care. I'll see you for a final check in five weeks. Then, if everything is healing OK, you can go back to your normal activities."

She came for her appointment after four weeks instead of five. "I feel so good, I just can't stand sitting around the house any longer," she told me. "I need to get back to work or I'll go stir crazy!"

With her head bowed, she looked at me and said, "I know you told me to take it easy but, two weeks after my operation, I went back to my usual routine of running several miles a day. My husband was ready to shoot me when he found out what I was doing, but I felt perfectly fine. After the first day, I just waited till after he left for work to go running so he wouldn't yell at me any more. I figured my body would tell me if I was doing anything that might hurt me."

With a sheepish grin on her face, she continued, "I know you wanted me to be careful of the incision on my stomach, but three weeks after surgery, I tried to do sit-ups and my belly felt fine. Since then I've been doing at least a hundred sit-ups every day. It didn't hurt so I couldn't see any reason not to."

Half expecting to find an incisional hernia because of the sit-ups, I was more than a little uneasy when I lifted the drape to examine her incision. What I saw was an incision that looked like it had been healing for months instead of just weeks.

Eventually, I decided it would be interesting to see what happened if my patients received Reiki treatments both before and after surgery. The first time I put this practice into effect was a morning when I had three major cases scheduled. I was just finishing the Reiki treatment on my first patient when a nurse approached with a big smile on her face. She seemed to be pretty excited about something. "Oh Dr. Mills, this is so wonderful! I'm a Healing Touch practitioner myself. Actually, there's a whole group of us here at the hospital. So far none of us has had the nerve to do any healing work on our patients. We were afraid the doctors would be disapprove. Seeing you do energy work in the hospital gives me hope that some day I'll be able to do it too."

"Well, you're always welcome to join me," I told her.

My second patient that day was a fifty-one-year-old woman who was scheduled to have an abdominal hysterectomy. I was surprised to find her alone when I opened the curtain to the cubicle where she waited lying on a narrow gurney.

Friends and family members were always encouraged to come into the pre-anesthesia area to wait with their loved ones until it was time for their operation. It helped the patients relax and made patients and family feel a little less frightened.

"Good morning," I said. "Are you by yourself today or has your husband just gone to the bathroom?"

Her hands worried the edge of the gown. Her jaw clenched for a moment then her face relaxed as she took a deep breath. Never quite achieving the casual tone she was aiming for, she answered in a strained voice, "Oh, he had to give a lecture at the medical school this morning. There really wasn't any reason for him to change his plans just to sit around the hospital waiting for me." She tried to smile but the smile never reached her eyes. "I'll be fine..." her voice broke on the last word.

Sitting on the edge of her bed, I held her shaking hand. "Yes," I assured her. "You will be fine. Do you have any more questions about the operation I'm going to do today?"

"No, you explained everything in the office. It's silly," she said, "I don't know why I'm so scared. Lots of women have hysterectomies." She impatiently wiped away a tear and continued, "My husband says I'm just being a big baby."

"No," I reassured her, draping an arm around her shoulder, "you're just being normal."

We chatted for a few minutes and then, after explaining what it was, I offered to give her a Reiki treatment. "It might help you to relax a bit," I told her.

"Thank you," she said. "I'd like that."

She lay back on the gurney and closed her eyes. I invited the Healing Touch nurse I had met that morning to join me and, together, we performed a healing on the woman.

By the time the anesthesiologist arrived to start my patient's I.V. and sedate her, the woman was so relaxed he had to rouse her to get her to hold her arm up for the I.V. She certainly didn't need medication to help her relax any more.

The same patient suffered from chronic headaches and routinely took narcotics to help control the pain. She later told me that when the nurse and I gave her the pre-operative Reiki treatment, her headache was completely relieved for the first time in months.

The last time I spoke with her, she told me that she and her husband intended to learn Reiki themselves, so she could stop using narcotics to relieve her headaches.

The memory of those days still leaves me in awe when I realize how the introduction of Reiki not only improved patients' immediate comfort but also profoundly changed so many people's lives.

CHAPTER SIX
College of Nursing

The next strand was woven into the tapestry when I was invited to give a lecture on the use of Reiki in medicine at the University of Arizona, College of Nursing.

When an idea is presented to students as part of their curriculum, they receive it with open minds. For this group of students, the idea that Reiki or another form of energy medicine would eventually be a part of their standard nursing care became an acceptable possibility.

Enough interest was generated within the group that I taught a special Reiki class for nursing students the following weekend.

Some months later, I received an excited phone call from Kelley, one of the student nurses who had attended that Reiki class.

While rotating through the neonatal intensive care unit, Kelley was assigned to assist in the care of a baby who had been exposed to cocaine in utero. Reiki turned what might have been a hopeless situation into a very positive experience for both the nursing student and the infant.

Because their condition is preventable, babies who have been exposed to cocaine are among the most heart-breaking cases in the nursery. These newborns startle at the lightest touch and any effort to comfort them leaves them frantic. A gentle cuddle in loving arms is intolerable to these babies. Captive in their personal agony, they remain inconsolable.

Kelley was changing the diaper on one of these tragic little people when, at her touch, the baby went rigid. The infant's body began to shake, and she screamed in misery. Having no idea what else to do for the baby, Kelley picked her up, placed her palms flat on the little back and allowed the Reiki to flow. The infant sighed and snuggled into Kelley's arms.

The instructor who was overseeing the nursing students that day told Kelley she must have a magic touch. Kelley just smiled.

May those who love us love us
For those who do not love us, may God turn their hearts
If he cannot turn their hearts then
may he turn their ankles
so that we may know them by their limping
~Celtic prayer

CHAPTER SEVEN

Fly in the Ointment

I believed it was my purpose to serve as a bridge between Eastern and Western medicine. In the hospital, I quietly introduced my patients and colleagues to Reiki, giving many mini-treatments. As I fixed people's headaches and minor aches and pains, the seeds of understanding and acceptance were planted in a very conservative medical community. Many people asked to "try it out" if only to see what all the gossip was about. If someone said, "No thank you," I backed off. Reiki is not about imposing my beliefs on someone else.

More often than not, my mini-treatments were a person's first personal exposure to any form of energy healing. I was amused when, after giving a brief treatment to one of the residents who had been up all night, he turned to me and said, "You're not going to believe this but I feel refreshed, like I've just had a nap."

I laughed. *I* never had any doubt that Reiki would make him feel better. *He* was the one who was surprised.

I love it when those things happen. It's such a gentle way for people to learn just what energy medicine is all about. The same young man later expressed an interest in learning Reiki.

There's a fine line between being an educator introducing new ideas to a community and an evangelist trying to impose her will on others. I was determined not to cross that line. I tried to be a gentle and respectful presence in the hospital. I just did my thing. If people were watching, that was fine with me. If no one was watching, that was OK too. If questioned, I taught. Reiki is a gift to be shared but only by those who desire it. My path is my path but it is not the only path.

Even in the best of circumstances, change is not introduced without a certain amount of resistance.

One day on labor wing, I admitted a patient I had seen in the office every week of her high-risk pregnancy. Angela was a lovely woman about my age. We had become quite close during her long, difficult pregnancy. One of her medical conditions, gestational diabetes, was causing her baby to become quite large. We decided to induce her labor before he got too big for a safe vaginal delivery.

Upon entering her hospital room, Angela's body began to tremble and tears streamed down her cheeks.

Gently stroking her back, I asked, "What's going on here?"

Her voice shook when she told me, "The last time I was in this hospital was the day my little three-year-old niece died here. When I walked into the hospital room, I had this awful vision of my own baby dying here today."

I held her hand, and we talked for a while. Eventually I offered her a Reiki treatment which she gratefully accepted.

Forty-five minutes later, she was calm and comfortable. I left the room to answer a page then returned to spend the rest of a very brief labor with Angela and her family. She had a lovely, healthy little boy. I was happy to have had the privilege to deliver a patient I knew well and thought of as a friend.

I thought everything had turned out quite perfect that day, however, as I would find out later, there had been one small fly in the ointment.

The next morning Angela told me, "I don't want you to be upset, but I just thought you ought to know what happened yesterday. As soon as you left the room after my Reiki treatment, the nurse came up to me with her hands on her hips and an angry expression on her face and she said, 'I just want you to know that sort of treatment is certainly not the standard of care in this institution. I hope you have not been offended by it.'"

"Well," Angela continued, "I looked that stupid woman right back in the eye and told her in a very firm voice, 'It certainly should be.'"

The barrier between doctors and staff was such that, though I was rarely challenged to my face, my nontraditional therapy was occasionally discussed in the nurses' lounge in a less than respectful manner. Or so I was informed by a nurse who was a friend of mine.

I shrugged my shoulders and accepted the information. I had opened some doors and planted some seeds. That made it all seem worthwhile to me. What saddened me was that three of the nurses who asked me to teach them Reiki ultimately chose not to come to my class because they were afraid of what their colleagues would say. Those nurses who did learn Reiki continue to use it covertly because of their fear of peer pressure.

Human nature being what it is, it is simply not possible to introduce a totally new and foreign concept to a large group of people without rocking a few boats. The fact that I was already an established member of the medical community, and that I never abandoned the practice of Western medicine, made my use of Reiki in the hospital a little more palatable for my conservative medical colleagues. Still, the work I did was not universally accepted.

Instead of being discouraged, I remind myself that I had a unique opportunity to serve as a bridge between the worlds of Western medicine and energy healing. My work served to open some minds and some hearts to one of the greatest gifts the universe has to offer. Hoping to recreate the world of Western medicine over night is an unrealistic expectation. I feel blessed for having been given the opportunity to help get things started.

CHAPTER EIGHT

In the Office

Once I began openly discussing hands-on healing work at the hospital, I started to talk about Reiki in our office as well. The Ob-Gyn department was a close knit group. The atmosphere in our office was both supportive and loving. At that time I was the only person in our five doctor, nine nurse office to be doing energy work or any sort of alternative healing.

Reactions were varied when I started telling my Reiki stories in the office. The nurses were respectful and indulgent. They liked me and enjoyed the stories. At first I don't think any of them actually believed I was channeling energy. I suspect they thought my patients felt better because I was a nice lady with a gentle touch and a comforting presence.

Attitudes began to change after I started to fix owies in the office. Initially they accepted my offers just to humor me. As each of them personally experienced Reiki, it was no longer a question of whether or not they believed me. They *knew* Reiki worked. Reiki became the first line of treatment for everyone's little aches and pains in our office.

I knew the tides had fully shifted the day Carol, one of the nurses, came into the nurses' station looking for Tylenol for a migraine. I offered her Reiki to fix her headache.

She said, "No thanks, I'll take the pills and if that doesn't work then I'll ask you later."

Suki, our head nurse, immediately turned to her and said, "Don't be silly, Carol. Let her give you Reiki. It will work much faster than the pills." And so she did.

I had always suspected that Judy, our nurse practitioner, was one of the non-believers until a couple days before she was scheduled to have surgery to remove a painful cyst from her wrist. She asked if I thought Reiki might shrink her cyst.

I said, "Sure, let's give it a try."

I ran energy on her wrist for about fifteen minutes. At one point the area became quite painful to her, but I was able to scoop away the pain with my hands. The cyst did indeed disappear. The operation was cancelled, and Judy was the first of my colleagues to learn Reiki. She still uses it to help relieve the arthritis pain in her father's hands.

The physicians' responses were more varied than the nurses'.

Jack never said anything one way or the other but he was always respectful towards me.

Elin came to my house for full Reiki treatments. She often asked me to work on her in the office when she was exhausted after a sleepless night on call. In spite of this, in the presence of our colleagues, she could never remember the name of "that thing Jeri does".

Joe openly mocked me. He laughed when patients told him how much they had benefited from Reiki treatments when they were in labor. He acted as though he thought we women were all just a bit silly.

One day, in an attempt to explain to Joe what energy work was all about, I showed him an exercise that I often teach in my beginning classes.

Standing at right a angle to Joe, I extended my right arm taking care that the elbow was not locked. I asked him to place his left hand on top of my biceps and his right hand on the underside of my forearm. After instructing him to try to bend my arm, I resisted his strength with my muscles. My arm shook with the effort but he was easily able to bend the arm.

We repeated the process, but this time, I used energy to strengthen my arm. Allowing the muscles to relax completely, I inhaled energy into my body and exhaled it through my arm. As the energy flowed out the fingertips of the extended hand, I visualized my arm turning into a rigid piece of steel. With no physical effort on my part, my arm became very strong and Joe was unable to bend it.

At the end of the demonstration, he had a slightly puzzled look on his face when he said, "Well, yes, there was a difference between the two experiences but I don't believe you were channeling energy. There must be some sort of trick involved." Shaking his head, he turned and walked away.

Alan was the most open minded of my physician colleagues. One day he told me in his quiet, gentle voice, "My wife is also interested in metaphysics but I, myself, am more scientific."

I was chatting with Suki and Susan at the nurses' station one day when Alan walked into the room wringing his hands

Alan is a large-boned man, about six foot three inches tall. The fair skin of his balding head is set off by a scant fringe of strawberry blonde hair. In contrast to his great size, his manner is soft spoken and reserved. He never seems to lose his temper, but when he's upset his very pale, very bald head turns fire-engine red. Alan's head was fire-engine red that day.

His beeper went off. Closing his eyes, he said in a disgruntled voice, "Oh, no. Not again! This crazy woman has been having me paged every half hour since I came on call this morning.

"Today is her due date and she keeps insisting that I induce her labor. I tried to explain that a due date is just an approximation of when she'll deliver. Her cervix isn't ripe yet and if I tried to induce her today, she'd probably end up with a C-section. Don't these people listen to anything we tell them in the office?"

I took his arm and guided him toward the nearest chair. "Sit down," I said.

After massaging the knots from his shoulders, I raised my hands to his temples and the Reiki began to flow. It seemed like only a few seconds had gone by when he gave a big sigh and his whole body relaxed.

He had a smile on his face as he said in a soft little voice, "It kind of lifts you up..."

Later that day he was overheard telling our partner, "Joe, you've got to try it. It was the most amazing thing. It's like I was floating."

Alan's wife attended my next Reiki class. She gave him Reiki treatments whenever he needed to destress. Several months later, Alan phoned me to say, "OK, I'm ready to learn now." And so he did.

CHAPTER NINE

Ohm

In November of 1995, I took the oral portion of my Ob-Gyn Board exam. All the candidates from the entire United States gathered in Chicago that week to undergo the ordeal.

Each candidate is assigned to a private room for the duration of the three-hour exam. At the start of each hour a bell rings and two examiners come into the room. They fire questions at the candidate for an hour. When the bell rings again, they leave the room to be replaced by two more examiners. The exam is notorious for being a baptism under fire. History tells us to expect intimidation tactics to be the rule, not the exception.

Prior to leaving for the exam, I asked many of my friends if they would please send energy for me at 1 P.M. (*the exam start time for me*) on the day in question.

A little before 1 P.M. on the exam day, approximately two hundred and fifty of us were herded into a large conference room. We were left there to wait for about half an hour before the powers that be came to speak to us about the test and send us off to our assigned rooms.

The air in the conference hall was thick with fear and anxiety. Two hundred and fifty careers rested on the results of the next three hours. The room hummed with the sound of people chatting nervously with each other. Others sat alone and I could see their lips move as they used the last few moments to review obscure facts and figures they feared might be asked in the questioning. The tension rose with each passing moment as we sat in the room and waited.

I decided the best place for me to be during the waiting period was somewhere else. Closing my eyes, I placed my hands on my solar plexus, my fear place, and allowed the Reiki to flow while I breathed myself into a meditative state.

Feeling peaceful and relaxed, I visualized myself sitting in a beautiful meadow of green grass and wild flowers. In my mind, I began to see the faces of the friends who had promised to send energy. They appeared one by one. As they approached me, my friends joined hands and formed a circle around me. Sitting in the midst of all the anxiety and chaos of the pre-exam room, I felt as though I was enclosed in a circle of love and support.

I was calm and relaxed when I walked to my assigned room.

I flew home that night after the exam. The following day, when I walked into the office, I was greeted with hugs of welcome.

Suki then told me, "Jeri, the strangest thing happened yesterday. Susan, Judy, and I were sitting together talking about you and how we hoped you'd do well on your exam. Then, at precisely 1 P.M., without talking about what we were going to do or how we would send you energy, we just all stood up, joined hands and began chanting 'Ohm...'"

It goes without saying, I passed the exam.

CHAPTER TEN

Intuition

One of the most important lessons I learned over the years is to trust my instincts, to listen to my visceral warning system, and to honor the information it presents to me.

During the winter and spring of 1996, my mare was boarded at a small stable near my house. There were only about ten horses on the property. The people I met there were all very pleasant, but struck me as a group of very traditional thinkers.

The first time I met Bob, he came to the stable to show my friend his new horse. We all admired the animal, a beautiful young Arabian, and then stood around just talking horses for a while. The conversation never became more personal than horse talk, so we really didn't become very well acquainted with one another.

The next time I saw Bob, he had just finished riding his friend's horse, a fractious young colt. It was a pretty uneventful ride until the horse suddenly started bucking like a rodeo pony. The man was launched across the arena and landed like a rag doll. When I saw him at the far side of the property, Bob was back on his feet, but he was hobbling around with a great deal of difficulty, dragging his left leg. His left arm was cradled in his right hand and, even from that distance, it was obvious that he was hurting.

My hands heated up and I had an overwhelming urge to offer assistance. The traditional part of my brain was in complete conflict with my Reiki Master self. This man, whom I barely knew, was a cowboy type with a Southern accent. I simply presumed he would be closed to any alternative healing methods. I suspected he might even think I was crazy if I offered to lay on hands to remove his pain.

After about a five second hesitation, my Reiki Master self won. I crossed the property and approached him. "I do this thing called Reiki." I told him. "It's an ancient hands-on healing technique that can accelerate healing and help control pain. I'd be glad to give you a treatment if you'd like one. I think it might make you more comfortable."

He didn't even hesitate. He smiled and said, "Oh, yeah, I believe in that stuff. A friend told me about it a few years ago."

He gingerly lowered himself into a chair, and I began to work on him. Before I touched him, he was unable to straighten his left knee and could just barely place any weight on the leg. He was also experiencing a lot of pain in his left forearm.

Scanning his energy field, the first thing I noticed was that about a third of the way between his elbow and wrist there was a place on his left arm that gave off a quick little puff of heat every time my hands moved over it. As long as I worked on the arm, the pain was controlled, but as soon as I removed my hands, the pain returned. I soon realized the little puff of heat was at the site of a fracture. This was confirmed a few days later when I finally convinced him to go see a doctor.

I worked on the leg for a half hour or so. At the end of the treatment, he had full range of motion of both hip and knee joint and was able to bear much more weight on the injured leg.

The following day I asked him to lie down on a bale of hay and gave him a full Reiki treatment. Before going home he stood on his left leg and jumped up and down on one foot to show me it was all better. Again, the pain in his arm was relieved while I ran energy through it but returned as soon as I removed my hands. The fracture needed to be stabilized so that the bones could knit.

The other boarders at the stable became curious after seeing the results of Bob's Reiki treatment. I finally felt free to speak openly about Reiki. Over the next few weeks, I gave several people Reiki treatments on my makeshift massage table of hay bales. I even used Reiki to relieve the belly pain in a colicky horse while we waited for the vet to arrive.

Had I ignored the spontaneous flow of Reiki from my hands and listened to my practical self, I might never have approached Bob. I presumed, because of a superficial first impression, that he would not be interested in Reiki. Not only did Bob receive great physical relief because of the treatment, he was to become my very first Reiki student.

The sensation of a puff of energy coming from a fracture site was to be demonstrated to me two more times in the next few months. The first time, one of our obstetric patients was admitted to the hospital after a motor vehicle accident. She had injuries to her arm, leg, and knee. Scanning her energy field, I felt a little puff of energy at the exact spot where a fracture site was identified on a radiograph an hour later. As with Bob, the fracture pain was relieved as long as my hands were on her arm but returned the moment I removed them.

The third time I perceived the same kind of energy signal, I was at another stable. A little girl had been thrown from her pony. It was late afternoon and everyone was tired and cranky. Her mother was certain the child was just whining to get attention. She decided to take her daughter home, have dinner, and forget about the whole thing.

My hands heated up. Listening to my body, I approached the crying child and asked if she would like me to do some Reiki on her arm to try to make her feel better.

"OK," she sniffed through her tears.

Again, I felt the little puff of energy as I scanned her arm. She relaxed and the tears stopped while my hands were over the site. "It's getting better," she said.

As soon as my hands were removed, the tears returned and she wailed, "Owww... It hurts."

I was able to convince the woman to take her daughter to the emergency room where a radial fracture was diagnosed and treated.

In general, I do not recommend that one attempt to make a medical diagnosis with Reiki. As healers, we are interacting with a person's energy field. What we perceive may or may not correlate with specific conditions of her physical body. Our energetic perception may also relate to past or future physical conditions. Trying to practice medicine via Reiki can be very dangerous. It is also illegal.

Be that as it may, when a healer becomes more experienced, certain signs will lead her to suspect the presence of specific injuries or conditions of the physical body. In these circumstances I believe it is the healer's responsibility to encourage her client to seek medical care.

If the problem I encounter in a healing session is something as simple as a broken bone, I believe it's perfectly acceptable to say, "I think there may be a fracture here. I wish you would get it checked out."

For less obvious or more serious problems, I usually handle the situation by telling my client that a certain part of her body seems to be drawing an inordinate amount of energy. I suggest that she see her physician to make sure there isn't a problem in that area. Even when I believe I know exactly what's going on, I rarely offer a diagnosis. With my healer hat on, I feel it's not my place to do so.

One must also have the sensitivity to realize that blurting out something like, "I think there's a cancer in your ovaries," creates terror. Without absolute certainty of the diagnosis, it would be cruel and harmful to place such fear into someone.

Sending a client for medical care is by no means a decision that marks the end of a healer's work with that client. Far from it. I simply believe there are situations that respond better to a combination of Eastern and Western medicine than to either venue alone. I think it would be irresponsible and arrogant of us to deny our clients the opportunity to explore every possible means of care available to them.

As healers we must trust our instincts. We should never ignore information that is made available to us. It is essential that we use kindness, discretion and wisdom when we decide what to do with the information we have received. We must also remember the primary goal of healers and physicians alike, "First, cause no harm".

CHAPTER ELEVEN
Healing Pets

Having been a small animal veterinarian in the past, and living in a house filled with pets, it goes without saying that I have had many occasions to offer Reiki to small animals. Puppies, kittens, and geriatric dogs and cats have all benefited from energy treatments.

Some of the animals only wanted Reiki when they were frightened or ill. Others, like my old cat Kelley, became positive Reiki addicts. Whenever I taught a Reiki class, Kelley spent the entire day in the room with us. If someone was on the massage table for a treatment, Kelley would plant himself on that person's stomach the entire time if he we let him. We were never completely sure whether the cat was receiving a treatment or helping to administer one.

I adopted Chuckie the puppy from the dog pound. As soon as we got home, I placed the sickly pup on my lap and began giving him a Reiki treatment. Kelley immediately joined us. The old cat gently lay down on top of Chuckie and placed his little paws on the dog's head. I was sure Kelley helped to give the treatment that night.

It was Labor Day, 1997. I had just put my horse up in her stall and was getting ready to head home when my friend Jennifer came into the barn. She seemed a little worried.

"Oh, Jeri, I'm glad you're still here," she said. "I was hiking out in the desert this morning and found a puppy wandering around by herself. She's in pretty rough shape. She's so weak she can barely walk, and I think she may be blind. It may be too late to save her, but I couldn't just leave her there."

She looked at me a little sheepishly. "Would you mind taking a look at her for me? My vet's office is closed for the holiday and I hate to pay to take the pup to the emergency clinic if you think she doesn't have a chance. Still, I don't want to drop her off at the pound either. I know they'd just kill her there because she's sick."

I followed Jennifer to her car. She opened the door and cringing in the back seat was one of the most pitiful scraps of life I'd ever seen. I was looking at what appeared to be little more than a skeleton loosely draped in an over-large coat of brittle, fawn colored hair. The creature's eyes were obscured by a thick, purulent discharge. I lifted the puppy out of the car. Her little body sagged in my arms. When I gently lifted and then released the fold of skin at the back of the pup's neck, it stayed tented in the air. The pup was too dehydrated for her skin to fall back into its normal position.

"Do you think it has eyes?" she asked anxiously.

I wiped the puppy's eyes with a damp cloth. Once the thick coating had been removed, her eyes looked surprisingly healthy. I decided the discharge had probably formed because she was too dehydrated to make tears.

The little dog tilted her head towards me, and I was struck by the jaunty angle of her ears. They seemed to promise hope for this woebegone little creature.

"Would she drink any water for you, Jen?"

"Oh!" she looked embarrassed, "I never thought to offer her any."

I set the puppy on the ground in front of the plastic bowl Jen had filled with about a pint of water. The dog perked up immediately. Once she started drinking, she didn't lift her head until the bowl was empty. When she finished her water, the little creature seemed to wilt in front of me as if the effort of drinking had drained her last reserve of energy.

I picked the puppy up. She lay her head on my shoulder, gave a long sigh, and snuggled tightly against my chest. My heart swelled.

"I'm not allowed to have dogs at my apartment," Jennifer informed me. "Do you think you could keep her till we can find her a home?"

The puppy barely moved as I carried her to my car and drove the ten miles to my house. When we arrived, I lay on the bed and set the sick puppy on my chest. The instant I placed my hands over her bony back, the healing energy began to flow. I dozed off. When I woke two hours later, the pup still slept on my chest and the Reiki was still flowing.

I took the pup outside to relieve herself and then offered her food and water. She was still too sick to eat but had a nice, long drink. When she was through, we returned to my room. I lay down and plopped her back on my chest. As soon as my hands approached the little body, it drew the Reiki from my hands like a vacuum cleaner. The energy was still moving hours later when we woke for our second trip outside. We repeated the process alternating Reiki-filled naps with brief trips outside. At 1 A.M., the Reiki stopped flowing.

The sickly little creature I brought home had been transformed into the most active puppy ever to enter my household. She kept the rest of us all up all night with her antics.

To this day, Katie-dog rules my house and outruns all the horses in the yard.

Yolanda, a good friend, and also one of my Reiki students, has found Reiki to be useful in treating her pet too.

When he was just a small pup, Yolanda's dog, Sabino, contracted Valley Fever, a potentially fatal systemic fungal infection. Valley Fever initially causes fatigue and weight loss in dogs. Untreated, it can form masses in the lungs and kidneys and may also invade the bones resulting in degenerative arthritis. In addition, it can infect the central nervous system resulting in behavior changes and seizures.

Sabino was treated with traditional therapy for over a year. The dog did well enough on medication, but as soon as he was taken off the drugs, his disease returned. Eventually, he developed so many side effects from the medication that Yolanda was afraid that if the dog didn't die from the disease, he just might die from the treatment.

Finally, she decided to replace the toxic drugs with daily Reiki treatments and Chinese herbs. The dog's symptoms completely disappeared. Sabino continues to receive regular Reiki treatments from his loving owner. He remains happy and healthy over three years later.

One day, I was petting my Great Dane, Heather, when I noticed a lump about two inches in diameter firmly affixed to the muscle over her right shoulder. With a sick feeling in my gut, I phoned my friend Debbie, a small animal veterinarian. "Debbie," I said, "I just felt a mass on Heather and I'm sure it's a malignant sarcoma."

"Now, Jeri," she replied, "you know we vets always expect the worst of everything. Before you work yourself into a panic, bring her into the office and I'll biopsy the thing. It's probably nothing."

I took Heather in for the biopsy. When we returned home, I started giving the dog Reiki. She came to me frequently over the next few days and lay patiently at my side while she received her treatments.

About three days later I had a call from Debbie. "Jeri," she said in a subdued voice, "I just got the pathology report back. You were right. Heather has a sarcoma. I think you should bring her in right away. I'll operate and try to remove the tumor. If the cancer hasn't already spread to her lungs, the dog might have a chance."

I ran my hand over Heather's shoulder. "I can bring her in, Deb, but I'm not sure you'll know where to cut. The tumor has completely disappeared!"

CHAPTER TWELVE

At The Ranch

There were over eighty horses at the ranch where I moved my mare in the summer of 1996. Prior to that time, I had used Reiki primarily to treat humans and knew little about the energy system of horses. My own mare, Abbie, was never terribly interested in receiving Reiki.

At the ranch, there were a lot of performance horses, hunter jumpers, dressage, and endurance horses. These animals frequently suffered minor injuries as a human athlete would. Their owners were always looking for new ways to help them. What a golden opportunity for me!

After becoming acquainted with a few women at the ranch, I explained what Reiki was and asked if I might practice on their horses. I told them I could not guarantee miracle cures, but I could assure them that Reiki would cause no harm.

I worked on a number of horses fairly regularly. Some horses didn't draw much energy. Others were positive energy sponges. All would relax. Many exhibited the drooping eyelids and twitching lips indicative of horsey ecstasy. When I worked on a horse in one of the open areas of the property, it was not uncommon for other horses who were passing by with their riders to veer towards me and lean their heads over my shoulder as if to say, "I want some of that too."

One little girl asked me to work on her big hunter whenever his back was sore. As soon as my hands touched his back, the horse would give a loud sigh, drop his head, and close his eyes. His little girl would giggle. He always performed better for a few days after those sessions.

My own mare, who was still quite young at that time, was terrified one day when a mounting block tipped over while I was climbing onto her back. After that, she developed the dangerous habit of bolting whenever I tried to mount her. I frequently watched hooves rush past my head as I lay on the ground.

With lots of patience and the help of my riding teacher, we got Abbie over the worst of that habit. She still became tense when I mounted until the day I discovered that a five minute Reiki treatment administered just before riding left my mare calm and relaxed. Her old fears were forgotten and the dangerous behavior never returned.

To this day, Abbie will rarely accept Reiki when she's sore but soaks it up like a sponge when she's nervous or upset.

My most heart-warming experience in equine energy work involved Val, an old quarter horse. Val was being leased by some well-meaning but inexperienced horse people.

A few days after her arrival at the ranch, Val was cast in her stall. While lying down, she rolled under the rails and became trapped. By the time she had freed herself, her body was a mass of cuts and abrasions. A deep gash filled with dried blood arced over her left hip. Shredded bits of torn skin dangled from her hocks and her left shoulder had swollen to twice its normal dimensions.

A vet was called to see to her injuries. Even though the man was not trained in equine chiropractic, he attempted to adjust the horse's neck. By the time he finished with her, Val was no longer able to straighten her neck. She stood with her front legs apart, working valiantly to retain her balance. Her condition continued to deteriorate with each passing day. The people who were leasing her stopped visiting because it made them feel bad to see her in such a terrible state. Val received no further medical care.

For two weeks, the mare remained in her stall, fed and watered but otherwise ignored. She stood with her right hip dropped about six inches lower than her left. Her neck curved around to her right side and her head tilted to one side at an odd angle from her neck. Pain prevented her from lifting her head higher than the junction of her legs and chest, about three feet. When she tried to turn quickly, she fell down. It was heartbreaking to see.

Finally, I couldn't stand to watch the creature suffer any longer. I asked Jim, the owner of the stable, if he thought it would be OK for me to give the horse a Reiki treatment. He shrugged his shoulders and said he didn't see why not since I "wouldn't really be doing anything to the mare except touching her".

I went into the stall and started Val's first Reiki treatment. Gradually, her stiff muscles began to relax under my hands. Her breathing became less labored and the haunted expression left her eyes. After about forty-five minutes, deciding she had enough for one day, I turned to leave the stall. The horse tried to follow me. In her urgency to stay at my side, she turned too quickly. Swaying on unsteady legs, it looked like the slightest breeze would knock her to the ground. The sight brought tears to my eyes. I stayed and continued to work on her for another forty-five minutes. When I left her stall, Val walked to the rails with a slow but steady gait, lifted her head to the top rail, about five feet high, grabbed it between her teeth, and started to stretch her neck.

I was thrilled with the improvement she had shown after just one session. Jim thought I was deluding myself.

I continued to work on Val for about an hour each day. At the end of a week, the mare's hips were level and the bend in her neck was almost gone. She was moving all four legs with ease, walking around the stall without threat of falling. Even Jim was impressed by the change in her.

The next day, the owner, who had not seen Val since before the injury occurred, phoned to say she was sending a vet to euthanize the horse. Appalled, Jim assured her the horse was much better. It took a while, but he finally convinced her to come out and see for herself before having the mare put down.

Jim and I were standing with Val when the owner arrived with her vet. They both acknowledged that the horse was much improved. The owner decided that even though Val's condition was improving, it would take a long time and more money than she felt the horse was worth to continue to feed and board her during her convalescence. She still intended to have Val euthanized.

I was devastated. Jim stepped in and offered to keep the horse himself rather than have her killed. The owner finally agreed. Jim gave the mare room and board, and I continued to work on her every day. At the end of a month, Val still had a slight head tilt, but she was sound and bounding with energy as she cantered through the fields.

Horses are easy to treat. They have no preconceived notions to overcome before accepting a Reiki treatment. Humans are a bit more difficult. There are, however, enough falls and human injuries occurring every day at an eighty-horse stable to provide ample opportunities to introduce Reiki to humans.

At first, I just offered to fix owies when someone had been thrown from a horse. After a while, riders began to ask me for Reiki treatments to relieve sore backs or other aches and pains prior to taking a lesson or riding in a show class. We used Reiki to treat everything from sprained ankles to menstrual cramps to the itching from a case of hives. Reiki could do it all.

A number of riders asked me to teach them Reiki. Eventually, there were eight Reiki practitioners on the property. That was almost ten percent of the human population!

Reiki became commonplace at the ranch. For a long time, I was too naive to realize that even in a setting where Reiki had been openly practiced on horse and human alike for months, some people were still skeptical. The point was brought home when I spoke with Jim the morning after his wife attended my Reiki class. Knowing that she had given Jim his first Reiki treatment the previous evening, I asked him if he liked it.

He looked a little surprised as he answered, "You know, it works. It relieved the pain in my shoulders."

"But Jim," I replied, "you've been seeing the results of Reiki treatments on horses and riders for months now. Why are you surprised?"

"Sure," he answered, "but I never thought it would work on *me*."

Another day, Lynn, a woman I had never been particularly friendly with, was bucked off her horse. She had a headache and her neck was stiff with pain. In spite of this, she felt she had to work with the colt a bit longer after his misbehavior before she could put him up for the night. I offered her Reiki and, to my surprise, she accepted.

After a brief Reiki treatment, she turned to me with a dazed expression on her face and said, "The pain is gone."

"Well of course it is, what did you expect?" I replied.

She answered, "But I don't believe in this sort of thing so I really never thought it would work on *me*." Lynn finished working with her horse. From that day on, she and I were friends.

One evening, standing outside in front of the tack room, I was asked to give Reiki to a little eight-year-old girl with ADHD (*attention deficit hyperactivity disorder*). Amanda was zipping around the stable yard like a little hummingbird. Her mother caught her as she raced by. The child was still chattering away when they joined me near the hitching post where their mare was tied.

With my hands at her temples, the nervous buzz gradually stilled in the child. Taut shoulders began to relax and eyelids slowly drooped over her enormous blue eyes. She had just finished telling us "how cool it felt" when a group of four little girls walked up. I cringed, expecting that the children, being children, would make some cruel comment and Amanda, who was benefiting from the Reiki, would no longer accept the treatment. Ah, we of little faith...

"What are you doing?" one little girl inquired.

Before I could respond to her question, another child said, "Oh, that's just Reiki. My grandma does it too."

"What's that?" the first child asked.

I told her, "Oh, I'm just running energy."

"Cool," she said as she turned to her friends. "Let's go play over there."

It had finally happened. The day had arrived when seeing someone receive a Reiki treatment was as casually accepted at the ranch as seeing someone groom her horse.

PART TWO

Energy Medicine

*We thrive and we heal in ecstatic moments
when our spirits become stronger than our bodies
and our bodies respond
to the commands of our spirits.*
~Anatomy of the Spirit
by Caroline Myss

CHAPTER THIRTEEN

The Difference Between Healing and Cure

When I teach a first degree Reiki class, or Energy 101 as I fondly refer to it, I want my students to leave with the understanding that Reiki, or any other form of energy work, is not just a substitute for pain pills and surgery. It is a holistic system for healing the body, mind, and spirit.

The basis of energy medicine is the belief that disease of the physical body is a reflection of imbalances of the energetic body. These imbalances are often the result of unresolved emotional issues or traumas from the present or previous lifetimes. Left unresolved, these negative emotions remain trapped in a person's energy field. Eventually, they manifest as physical or psychiatric disease.

When the energetic cause of disease is removed, the physical body will often return to normal function. This is by no means the only positive outcome of a healing. Reiki is as capable of healing a broken relationship as a broken foot. When the emotional trauma associated with a physical condition is resolved, the person will benefit whether or not physical function is regained.

When Sarah first came to me to learn Reiki, her mother laughed and told her she was wasting her time. A few weeks later, her mother strained her back working in the garden. Sarah gave her a Reiki treatment, and to the old woman's consternation, it actually made her feel better. Still, she rarely asked her daughter to give her Reiki.

The following year, when Sarah was in France on a work assignment, her mother was diagnosed with lung cancer. Sarah sent distance healing to her mother each day while the older woman received chemotherapy and radiation treatments. Sarah later told me she could feel the tumor getting smaller when she sent the daily Reiki treatments. The doctors reported that the tumor was, indeed, shrinking.

Shortly after my friend returned to the States, her mother developed complications that made it necessary to discontinue the chemotherapy. At that time, her mother was also experiencing tremendous bone pain, a result of the injections she received to stimulate her bone marrow to produce red blood cells.

Sarah and her mother had always had a very turbulent relationship. The older woman constantly found reasons to criticize and berate my friend. When she first became ill, the mother was resistant to having her daughter do hands-on healing for her. The woman who, less than a year earlier, had scoffed at Sarah for learning Reiki did, however, ask to be brought to me for a treatment.

I worked on Sarah's mother for an hour or so. The next day, she told Sarah the Reiki gave her better pain control than Percocet, a fairly powerful pain medication, and the relief lasted for over twenty-four hours after the healing. After that, the old woman forgot her previous reservations and asked her daughter to give her daily Reiki treatments.

Each day, Sarah gave her mother a treatment. The cancer did not go away but two very important things did happen. First, Reiki was helpful in relieving pain for the dying woman. Second, and in my mind of even greater importance, Reiki healed the relationship between mother and daughter. What had been a turbulent, frequently angry relationship for over forty years became a close, loving bond between mother and daughter. The memory of those warm interactions will comfort my friend for the rest of her life.

In the summer of 1996 I attended an integrative medicine conference in Findhorn, Scotland. During the course of the main conference, Dr. Steve Wright, one of the Therapeutic Touch instructors, was asked to introduce himself. He slowly unfolded his lanky six foot four inch frame and faced the assembly. His wavy black hair and long lashed, brown eyes seemed more suited to a movie star than to the director of nursing of a geriatric ward in an English hospital.

In a soft, gentle voice, Steve told us a little about the hands-on healing system of Therapeutic Touch. To illustrate how the holistic approach to healing differs from the contemporary medical model of fixing the broken parts to effect a cure, Steve shared the following true story which he has graciously allowed me to retell.

Maevis had never been a large woman, but at ninety-four, time had put a curve in her spine and softened her bones until she was barely four feet ten inches tall. The cancer that had been eating away at her for many months had left her too weak even to lift her slight frame from a bedside chair without assistance.

As Steve stood in front of Maevis with his arms under hers and carefully eased the old woman to her feet, another nurse steadied her from behind. Standing supported in his arms, the old lady looked up at Steve with the hint of a smile on her lips and the glimmer of long forgotten memories shining in her eyes and said, "This reminds me of times when I was a wee lass... Me da would hold me in his arms and dance with me."

Still supporting the old woman, Steve turned to the other nurse and asked her to place the old woman's feet on top of his toes. The nurse's head snapped to attention. Her jaw dropped and she stared at him with an incredulous expression on her face.

Oh well, she thought, Stephen was, after all, her boss and though he was prone to doing things that were, in her opinion, a bit odd at times, he had never harmed anyone. So she shrugged her shoulders and complied with his wish, placing the old woman's feet on top of Stephen's toes.

Steve gathered the old woman up in his arms, began to hum a little tune, and started waltzing around the room. He held the old woman tenderly in his arms, her feet upon his feet, as a father might hold his small daughter when he lovingly shares a first dance with her.

After a few turns around the room, Stephen returned the old woman to her bedside, carefully helped her into the bed, and gently tucked the covers up under her chin.

The old woman looked up at Steve with a radiant smile on her lips, tears of joy and remembrance shining in her eyes and she said, "Thank you."

A short time later, the old woman closed her eyes and drifted off into a peaceful sleep. Later that day, her spirit left her body and she died. HEALED.

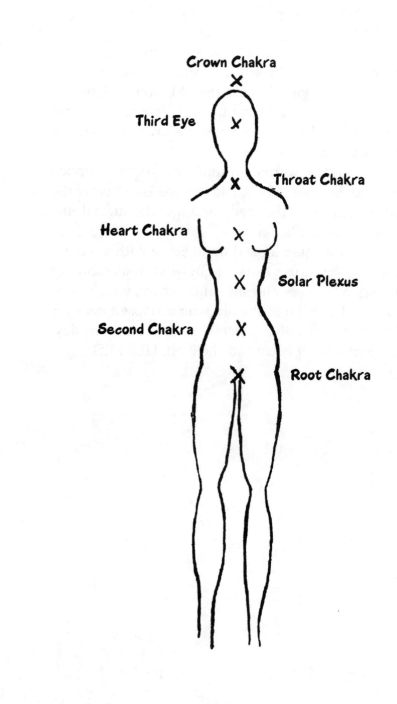

CHAPTER FOURTEEN

The Human Energy Field

Energy Medicine defines the human body as a physical core surrounded by concentric shells of energy. The structure is not unlike that of a set of Russian nesting dolls. The central core is the physical body. It is surrounded by the etheric or energy body which is composed of several layers. The layer closest to the physical body is an energetic layer known as the mental body. Still farther out lies the emotional body and at the periphery of our being is the spiritual body.

These layers are not fixed and rigid like our physical body. Their depth and breadth vary depending on our physical, mental, and emotional state at any given moment. When someone sees our aura, they are seeing a physical manifestation of our energy body.

Variations in the color, shape, depth, and breadth of the aura reflect our physical health and well-being as well as the state of our emotions. When we feel shy or uncertain, we can pull our energy bodies in so closely to our physical being that people may not even notice our presence in a room. At that moment our aura is a tight, little shell of light that closely adheres to our physical form. When we are filled with joy and self-confidence, the depth and breadth of our energy body is as expansive as our emotions. We can light up a whole room.

The physical body is divided into a series of major and minor energy centers known as chakras. The word chakra means wheel. Each chakra is a wheel or vortex of rotating light that occupies a specific location in the human body. The state of each chakra reflects the condition of associated parts of the anatomy and also specific categories of emotions that find their focus in that area of the body. An imbalance in the mental, emotional, or spiritual level of the energy body, if left unresolved, may eventually manifest as physical disease. Likewise, a physical injury will result in changes in corresponding areas of the energy body and the appearance of the aura.

There are seven major chakras. The first chakra, the root chakra, is located about four inches below the junction of the thighs just below the genitals. Its color is red. It is the site of the most primal emotions, of survival issues. The will to live or die is mirrored by the condition of the first chakra. Associated physical organs include the kidneys, the bladder, and the spine.

The second chakra is located in the center of the lower abdomen about two inches below the navel. Its color is orange. It is the center of sexuality and creativity. It can reflect personal issues as well as how we see ourselves in the context of the morality of the culture in which we live. Associated physical organs include the sexual organs, the pelvis, and the hips.

The third chakra is located at the solar plexus just below the lower end of the breast bone. Its color is bright yellow. It is the seat of our sense of power. It also reflects issues involving the opposite of power which is fear or a lack of self-confidence. Associated physical organs include the stomach, the spleen, the liver, and the adrenal glands.

The fourth chakra, the heart chakra, is located in the center of the chest. Its color is pink or green. It is the center of love. It is injured by the opposite emotions of love which are anger and fear. Associated physical organs include the heart, the lungs, and the thymus gland which is the governor of the immune system.

The fifth chakra, the throat chakra, is located at the base of the neck. Its color is light blue. It is the center that facilitates communication between the lower, more primal centers of survival and instinct with the higher intuitive and spiritual centers of our being. When we are afraid or unable to express our thoughts or emotions, the fifth chakra is blocked and we feel as though we are choking. Associated physical organs include the thyroid and parathyroid glands.

The sixth chakra, the third eye, lies in the center of the forehead between the eyebrows. It is the center of intuition, perception and clairvoyance. Its color is deep amethyst purple. It connects us with our higher selves. Associated physical structures include the autonomic nervous system which governs the body's responses to feelings of safety or fear.

The seventh chakra, the crown chakra, is located at the top of the head. Its color is golden. It is our connection with Spirit, the center of wisdom and unconditional love.

When performing a healing, we must keep in mind that it is the energy body that is being directly affected by our work. As Westerners, we have come to expect the result of a treatment session to be physical relief. Though improvement of physical structure and function often result from relieving imbalances of the energy body, as energy workers we must understand that as long as there has been an improvement in the mental, emotional, or spiritual well-being of the subject, the healing has been successful The purpose of a given lifetime may not be to achieve perfect physical function and longevity. A lifetime may be devoted to the attainment of peace and enlightenment of the spirit.

CHAPTER FIFTEEN
Intent and Belief

About an hour into a Reiki class, there is usually at least one face in the room looking at me with skepticism if not down right disbelief. "How," that person asks, "can an educated woman, a scientist, be spouting this airy fairy stuff?"

Were I an expert in quantum physics, I could offer a concise, scientific explanation of why energy medicine works. Since I am no physicist, here's the best explanation I can muster.

Most people know enough basic physics to understand that everything in the physical universe is made up of atoms and molecules. Atoms are nothing more than little solar systems comprised of a central core of positively charged energy particles surrounded by a swarm of negatively charged energy particles. So when we break it all down to the smallest identifiable parts, the physical universe is not "physical" at all. It's a conglomeration of negative and positively charged energy particles arranged in such a way that our senses perceive them as matter.

We can make these systems change their physical form when we alter the energy in them. If we add energy in the form of heat to water, it becomes steam. If we remove energy from water, it becomes ice. Thus, changing the energy of the system results in physical changes that are easily perceived by our five senses.

Now, let's take this one step further. What happens when you breathe? You use your mind to direct your diaphragm to move in a way that causes air to be drawn through your trachea and into your lungs. The diaphragm is made up of a combination of energy particles grouped together into a pattern we perceive as muscle. The air we inhale is a collection of energy particles in specific arrangements we identify as oxygen, nitrogen and carbon dioxide. In essence, the act of breathing is the act of using your mind, your intent, to move energy: your diaphragm and air.

Once it is understood that physical matter is no more than a specialized arrangement of energy particles, it becomes clear that every physical act we perform is actually an instance where we are using our intent to move energy.

The concept of using your intent to inhale healing energy through the top of your head or to exhale it through the palms of your hands suddenly becomes no more exotic than the act of breathing.

We have all experienced situations where intent has proven to be more powerful than physical forces. Remember the last time you tried to remove a small object from the hand of a two-year-old child? Your intellect tells you that your hand is much stronger than the hand of a toddler, so the task should be easy. It isn't. No one has taught the toddler that you are physically stronger than he is. It is his intent that the object remain in his palm. His intent has not yet been weakened by your beliefs, so you struggle to open the fingers of the child.

Now, remember the last time you removed an object from the hand of a six-year-old. This child has been told that you are stronger than he is. He *believes* this to be true and so it *is* true. The object is removed with relative ease.

Picture a Karate Master using his hand to break a pile of bricks. Are the flesh and bones of this man's hand stronger and harder than the bricks? No way. What *is* stronger than the bricks is his focused intent and belief that his hand will separate the bricks without being injured.

I used the example of the Karate Master in a Reiki class where two of my students happened to be men who had black belts in Karate. One of them looked at me and laughed as he said, "You're right. The time I let myself think of something else while I was breaking a board was the time I broke my hand instead of the board."

After this discussion, it's not uncommon for a student to turn to me and say, "OK, so maybe you can move energy with your mind but where does this *healing* energy come from?"

Personally, I've always favored the idea that we live in a benevolent universe and that healing energy is everywhere. We only have to learn how to gather it up. For those who require a bit more science, I relate some information that was presented at a seminar I recently attended.

The speaker was discussing the changes that occur in the EEG recording of a person's brain waves when she transitions from a normal state of consciousness to a meditative state. As she enters into a meditative state, her brain waves slow down from a rate of twenty or thirty cycles per second to a rate of ten cycles per second. The meditative state is similar to the level of consciousness achieved by Shamans when they journey and when they perform healings. The speaker further related that ten cycle per second energy frequencies have been recorded in healing chambers in the great pyramids. He then told us there is a level in the atmosphere of the earth where the energy frequencies are ten cycles per second.

As he made his final statement, something suddenly clicked in my mind. Perhaps this level of the earth's atmosphere is the Reiki source.

CHAPTER SIXTEEN

Shielding

Emotions are contagious. Picture a crowd that has gathered for a peaceful demonstration. A man with a dissenting point of view arrives and insults someone in the crowd. The two begin to argue and a fight breaks out. Only a handful of people have heard what was said. In spite of this, anger spreads through the crowd like wildfire and a riot breaks out.

A group of people gather to hear the Dahli Lama or the Pope. Most of the people don't know each other. Each person arrives carrying the emotional burdens of the day, an argument with a family member, a problem at work, worry over financial difficulties. People jostle each other to get the best seat. Each individual is involved with his own thoughts. Strangers don't make eye contact with each other.

The speaker arrives and delivers his message. His very presence radiates love and compassion. By the time he leaves the podium, the crowd is relaxed and peaceful. People feel connected. Strangers smile at one another and some of them reach out to shake hands or even to hug each other. At least for a little while, the burdens of the day have been forgotten, replaced with the feelings of love and understanding that have spread throughout the assembly.

After realizing that emotions can be contagious, it becomes obvious that a healer must be in a clear and loving state of mind when she lays on hands to perform a healing, or she might risk contaminating the client with her negative emotions. She must also find some way to protect herself from picking up her client's pain or distress.

If she uses pure Reiki for her treatment, there is a one way flow of energy from the universe through the healer's Reiki channels to the client. No one is at risk. If, however, there are other interactions between healer and client, be it a simple hug or the use of non-Reiki healing techniques, there is the possibility that an exchange of emotional energy will take place.

There are many ways a healer may prevent this exchange of negative energy from taking place. I routinely use several techniques to clear and shield myself from negative energy before leaving the house every morning, before teaching a class, and before laying on hands for a healing. The following are my favorite methods of shielding and protecting myself.

Clearing

Begin by taking a big, deep breath. As you inhale, imagine that you are drawing white light through your crown chakra into your head. As you exhale, use your breath to move the light down, through your body and finally direct it out through the soles of your feet and into the earth. As the light passes through you, *intend* that it carry away any negative energy that may be trapped inside your body. *Visualize* the negative energy leaving through the soles of your feet and draining deep into the center of the earth where it can be cleansed and recycled. Repeat this process three times.

Shielding

Visualize yourself being surrounded by of a silver bubble or force field. The bubble is selectively permeable. This means that only those things you choose to allow to move freely in and out of your bubble are able to do so. You don't want to put yourself inside a suit of armor because, though you would be protected from harm, you would be unable to receive or project love and healing. This is why it is essential to set the conditions for your bubble. The process is not unlike programming a computer. Decide what you want to be allowed to move freely through the barrier you are creating and what you want to be prevented from doing so.

I am very clear and specific when I define the parameters of my silver bubble. After using my intent to create the force field, I reinforce it with a series of affirmations. "I ask to be surrounded by a silver protective shield that will dissipate all negativity and harm. I ask to create a sanctuary of love, healing, wisdom, support (*and whatever else I may need in my personal sanctuary at that time*). I ask that it be freely permeable to the Reiki and to all loving, healing forces in the universe. I ask that it be protective of my vital life source energy (*my spirit*). I ask that it be open and welcoming to my loving spirit teachers and guides (*angels, higher power*)."

When in a location where I can do so without bringing unwanted attention upon myself, I speak my affirmations aloud. Doing so puts both the power of my intent and the energy of my voice behind my affirmations. As the Celts say, there is power in the word.

With shield in place and intent clearly defined, I am ready to start my day.

CHAPTER SEVENTEEN

Creating A Sacred Space

In the same way that negative emotions can spread through a crowd to infect other people, they can infect a room. Have you ever been in a place that gave you a prickly, uneasy feeling at the back of your neck? Can you think of some favorite place you visit as often as possible because it just feels good to be there?

I want my home to be the most peaceful and comforting environment possible. When someone comes into my home or my office, I want to invite them into a space that is warm, welcoming, and free from any lingering negative emotions. I want the energy of the place to be as clean as possible.

The traditions of most ancient cultures include a variety of rituals for cleansing and purifying environments to clear away negative energy and to create a sacred space. The use of ceremony and ritual helps us to focus our energies and to intensify them. Many believe that power comes from the ceremony itself, others believe that the power comes solely from the intent and belief of the person performing the ceremony.

My own spiritual beliefs have roots in Celtic, Native American and Buddhist traditions. The cleansing rituals that have power for me stem from these cultures. When I move into a new house or prepare my home for a special event, I perform the following rituals in the order that I am about to describe them. I tell my students to use any or all the methods, advising them to choose only those methods that feel good and right to them. A ceremony that has no meaning for the person performing it has no power.

Smudging

Smudging is a Native American practice that calls upon the spirit of sage or cedar to clear an environment of negative energy. As with any ritual, the intent and belief of the practitioner are the driving forces of the process.

Before starting my smudging ceremony, I turn on a tape of Native American flute music. The music helps put me into the correct frame of mind to perform this ceremony.

A door or window should be opened as an escape route for negative energy. It's also a good idea to turn off any smoke detectors in the house before performing this ritual.

To begin, hold a bunch of white sage that has been bound together into a smudge stick or else use a fire resistant pot filled with loose leaves of white sage. (*The pot should only be used for this purpose.*) Light the sage leaves. When they have all started to burn, blow out the flames so the leaves are left smoldering and smoking.

Walk slowly through each room allowing the smoke to fill the room and forcefully call out, "Spirit of the sage, Great Spirit *(Father, Mother, God)* I ask that you help me to cleanse this room and this house of all negative energies and entities. Banish from this space all that is not of love and of light. Purify this space and create a safe and loving sanctuary for learning, for healing, for ... (*Choose your own words here. Your request will vary according to what is about to take place in the room.)* End by saying, "I thank you Great Spirit." Move on to the next room and repeat the process. After smudging each room in the house, go outside and walk around the property smudging and clearing the energy of the land.

When I have finished smudging, I set up a medicine wheel or recharge the one that is already in place.

Medicine Wheel

Most shamanic cultures use some form of circle to define their sacred space. The Druids performed many sacred rituals inside giant stone circles like the formation at Stonehenge. Away from these special places, they used sand or salt to cast a circle around themselves to create a protected space. The circle might be the location where magic was to be performed or it might simply represent an energetic shield around the campsite of a traveler. In Native American traditions, a circle of stones is also used to delineate sacred space, they call this a medicine wheel.

To create a medicine wheel, first set your intent, "I wish to create a sacred space for healing."

Next, prepare the location with a physical cleaning and a ritual of purification such as a smudging ceremony.

Now, establish the four directions, North, South, East and West. Decide where the boundaries of your sacred space, your medicine wheel, will be. Your medicine wheel may be just large enough for you to sit in, a place to come to meditate and to heal, or it may encompass your entire living space. Place a stone or crystal at the locations on the boundary of your medicine wheel that correspond to each of the four directions. Choose any type of stone or crystal that feels "right" to you. (I generally use rose quartz.) Follow your intuition and you will make the right choice.

You must now energize your stones. Beginning in the South, approach and face the stone. Inhale deeply. As you inhale, draw universal energy through your crown chakra and let it flow into your center. As you exhale, beam the energy from your third eye, your solar plexus and your hands into the stone. (Reiki practitioners may also beam the Power Symbol from their hands at this time.) Continue the process until you can see a change in the stone and you know that it is "full". When you know you are done, turn to the West. Proceed around the circle stopping to charge or energize each stone in turn. When you have charged the last stone, return to face the stone in the South.

Once the stones have been charged with energy, you need to connect the stones. Using your mind and your hands, reach up and draw a ribbon of healing energy from the universe into the room and connect it to the first stone. Connect each of the remaining stones to a similar energy ribbon. Next, draw an energy ribbon from one stone to the next as you move around the circle. SEE the energy connection forming between the stones as you direct your energy ribbon. You are shaping an enclosed column of light whose boundaries are defined by the placement of the stones. You have now opened a vortex of cleansing and purification. You have created a sacred space in which negative energy cannot exist.

While performing this process say, "Great Spirit, I ask that you help me to connect these stones, to create a vortex of healing. Banish all negative energies and entities. Create a space where only that which is of love and light may exist. I thank you, Great Spirit."

When you have finished, stand inside your medicine wheel. Take a moment to face each stone and give honor to that direction. Thank the spirits respectfully before taking your leave.

I have created a medicine wheel to encompass each of the major rooms in my home. When I go through my cleansing rituals before a class or as I prepare for a special occasion, I repeat the ceremony I have just described to re-establish and reinforce my sacred space.

Reiki Symbols

After reinforcing the medicine wheels that protect each room in my house, I perform a ceremony whose roots originate in Buddhist healing traditions. I place the Reiki symbols into the walls of each room. The symbols serve to purify the space, to create a place where the scope of healings may transcend time and space and to fill the room with the loving energy of Reiki (*See Chapter 24 for a detailed description.*)

To an observer it may seem out of place to follow a shamanic ritual with a ceremony that comes from an oriental healing system, but to me, it feels right and natural to perform the ceremony at this time.

When all the ceremonies have been performed and the energy of the room is clean, I ask that the room be blessed. Then, I ask for divine guidance to help me set my personal burdens aside so that I may be a clear and loving channel of healing. Finally, I humbly invite my loving spirit teachers and guides to enter my sacred space. If I am about to teach a class or see a client, I also invite the loving teachers and guides of my students or my client to assist at the class or the healing.

CHAPTER EIGHTEEN
The History of Reiki

Reiki is an ancient hands-on healing art. It was commonly used in Tibetan society two to three thousand years ago. As the practice of Buddhism came to encourage people to become more focused on the enlightenment of the spirit and less concerned with the condition of their physical body, many of the old healing traditions were forgotten.

In the mid-nineteenth century, Dr. Mikao Usui was the dean of a Christian college in Japan. One day, one of his students asked him if he believed literally in the bible. Dr. Usui replied, "Yes, of course I do."

The student then asked, "Sir, will you please explain the healings that the bible tells us have been performed by Christ?" Dr. Usui was unable to answer the question.

Feeling honor bound to be able to respond to the queries of his students, Dr. Usui quit his job and began a quest to find the answers, a quest that would shape the rest of his life. He went first to a Christian seminary where he studied for several years, but he was unable to find the answers in

Christian studies. Knowing that Buddha, like Christ, was reported to have been able to perform healings, Dr. Usui decided to go to Buddhist monasteries to look for the answer. For many years, he studied ancient documents searching for an explanation of the methods that might have been used by Buddha and Christ.

He finally found what he was looking for in some Tibetan Sutras (*ancient documents*) that were over twenty-five hundred years old, but he had no idea how to apply the information he had discovered.

One of his teachers, an ancient Buddhist monk, advised him to go to Mount Kuri Yama, the sacred mountain outside of Kyoto, Japan. He was told that if he fasted and meditated for twenty-one days at the top of the sacred mountain, the answers would be shown to him.

Dr. Usui went to the top of the mountain. He prayed and he meditated, and each evening at sunset he set aside a stone to mark the passing of another day. He had been on the mountain for twenty days and had not yet received any of the information he was searching for. On the morning of the twenty-first day, just before dawn, Dr. Usui saw a bright light rushing through the sky towards him. At first he was terrified by the sight, but then he became very calm and very still. He realized this was what he had been waiting for.

The light struck Dr. Usui in the center of his forehead. He saw a series of symbols appear before his eyes and heard a voice say, "Remember these symbols." And then he lost consciousness.

When Dr. Usui awoke, the sun was high in the sky. He realized he had just received what he had sought for so many years. In his elation, he jumped up and began running down the mountain. In his speed, he tripped on a stone and cut his foot. Without giving any thought to what he was doing, he reached down and placed his hand over the cut on his foot. His hand became burning hot, and the pain disappeared. When he removed his hand, the flow of blood had stopped and the cut was completely healed. His search had ended. Dr. Usui had received the ability to heal. He called this form of healing Reiki which in Japanese means universal life force energy.

Dr. Usui spent the next seven years of his life healing the inhabitants of the beggars' quarter in Kyoto, Japan. He believed that if he healed the physical ills of the beggars, they would be able to leave the beggars' quarter and have a more productive role in society.

After a while, he began to see familiar faces reappearing around him. One day, he stopped a young man and asked, "Don't I know you ?"

"Oh, yes, Grandfather," the young man replied. "I was one of the first people you healed. After that, I got a job, I went to the temple and received a name. I even took a wife. But my life was very stressful and I did not like it so I left my wife and my job and returned to the beggars' quarter to my old and easy life."

Dr. Usui was devastated. He felt like a failure. He prayed and he meditated and finally, he came to understand that he had failed because he had given healing energy to people who had neither requested nor desired the healing. They had also done nothing to participate in the process. He had passed it on to them like alms for the poor. He realized then that healing should only be provided for those who truly wanted it. He came to understand that for a healing to be complete, the recipient must value it enough to work for it. He must be willing to offer some form of payment or exchange of energy for the healing.

Dr. Usui spent the rest of his life traveling through Japan and healing those who sought him out. He carried a torch, lit even during daylight hours, to signify that he brought light and healing.

During this time, he discovered that the symbols he had been shone on the top of Mount Kuri Yama had three functions. He could use them during a healing to direct the flow of energy to the mental or emotional planes. He could use them to direct healing to a distant time or place. He also discovered that the symbols could be used to pass on the ability to perform Reiki healings to other people.

Dr. Usui instructed many Reiki healers throughout his lifetime. Before his death, he chose one man to become his successor. Dr. Usui taught this man how to pass on the ability to channel Reiki. This man was a retired Japanese naval officer named Dr. Chujiro Hayashi.

Dr. Hayashi opened the first Reiki clinic in Kyoto, Japan. It was there, in 1935, that a Hawaiian-born Japanese woman named Hawaya Takata, who had returned home to receive medical care for a serious illness, ultimately received treatment. She was so moved by the effects of Reiki that she asked to become one of Dr. Hayashi's students.

In exchange for Reiki training, Mrs. Takata worked in his clinic for two years. Dr. Hayashi taught Mrs. Takata until she had attained the level of training of what we now call a second degree Reiki practioner. Because she was a woman, he refused to advance her training any farther.

She returned to Hawaii and started her own Reiki clinic where she performed healings for many years.

Some time before the start of World War II, Dr. Hayashi had a premonition that there was to be a great war. He believed that he and all the men he had instructed as Reiki Masters would die as a result of that war. He knew that if knowledge of Reiki were to survive, he would have to teach women to be Reiki Masters. He chose his wife and Mrs. Takata for this honor.

His premonition did indeed come to pass. He and all the male Reiki Masters whom he had taught were dead by the end of the war. The only remaining Reiki Masters in the world were two women, his wife and Mrs. Takata. Mrs. Takata spent the rest of her life working in her healing clinic and teaching Reiki. Mrs. Hayashi chose never to teach. This means that all the Reiki practitioners in the world today are descendants of the students of Mrs. Takata.

Just for today do not worry
Just for today do not anger
Honor your teachers, parents and elders
Earn your living honestly
Show gratitude to all living things
~The Reiki Principles

CHAPTER NINETEEN

Learning Reiki

The Attunement Process

One of the things that makes Reiki unique among the various types of hands-on healing is the way in which it is taught. A person does not need to spend months in seclusion, years studying, or even learn how to meditate in order to learn Reiki. Reiki is taught using an attunement process. This attunement is achieved through the performance of an ancient ceremony or, as Paula Horan describes it in her book *Empowerment Through Reiki*, the use of ancient Tibetan technology that serves to open the student's Reiki channels to the flow of universal life force energy. Once these channels have been opened, the student has only to place her hands with the intent of healing and the Reiki will flow.

Once someone has been attuned, the ability to channel Reiki energy will remain with her for the rest of her life, even if she doesn't use it for a long time. As with most skills, the more someone uses Reiki the stronger it will become.

When a person receives a Reiki attunement, her channels are opened, however they may still be partially clogged by the negative energy of memories, thought forms and beliefs that she carries with her. As Reiki flows through her body, these negative energies are released and swept away from her Reiki channels. As the channels are cleansed by repeated use, the flow of Reiki becomes steadily stronger.

To help my students understand this process, I like to use the analogy of pouring a bottle of Drano into a blocked pipe. The initial application of chemicals opens the clog and allows water to begin to flow through the pipe. The instructions on the bottle of Drano tells us to run lots of hot water through the pipe to wash away the debris that has been loosened up by the chemicals. The more water we run through the pipe, the more debris is washed away and the more freely water can flow through the pipe. And so it is when the Reiki channels are opened and then swept clean by repeated use.

Reiki is a precious gift from the universe. It is available for us to use whenever it is needed. It saddens me to know that many Reiki students don't use their gift because they lack confidence or because, after neglecting to use their Reiki for a while, they assume it is not there any more. Reiki cannot be lost or taken away by outside forces.

Alice rarely used Reiki on herself and never used it on another person after her class. Three years later, when Alice's mother was dying from esophageal cancer, she decided to "try to give her mother a treatment".

"My mother's face was contorted with pain, her whole body was tense, and her breathing was fast and shallow," she told me. "It had been so long since the class that I couldn't even remember what to do. I just laid my hands on my mother and pictured white light. My hands heated up. All of a sudden there was an incredible change in my mom. Her face began to relax and her breathing slowed down as the pain went away.

"My mother and I were always very close. Once she was on morphine for the cancer, we couldn't talk very much any more. I knew the cancer was too far advanced to save her, but it gave me a special feeling to know that, at the very end, I could do something for my mother that my brothers and sisters couldn't do, something that made my mom feel better."

Even those of us who do use Reiki regularly may occasionally find ourselves in situations where we begin to wonder if the Reiki is still with us. I, myself, went through such a crisis of faith in the spring of 1996 after a shaman performed a healing on me. During the session he said some things that made me doubt my own abilities as a healer. Looking back, it's hard to believe that such a thing could have happened to me at that time. It was the most exciting and productive period of my life as a healer. I saw magic happen under my hands on a daily basis in the hospital. In spite of daily proof to the contrary, I was so in awe of the man that I allowed his negative comments to cloud my perceptions of myself and my abilities.

The culmination of this period of doubt arrived a few weeks later when I performed a healing on a woman during my trip to Findhorn, Scotland. For the first time, the healing work became a concentrated effort instead of the joyful extension of myself it had always been. Later that day I meditated on the problem and came to understand what was happening. The following entry was written in my journal a few days later:

"Going back to Findhorn, to the healing I did on Christina, I may have 'over done' some of the work.

I was working from my head instead of from my heart. I had, over the last weeks and for reasons I don't quite understand, become afraid that I had lost my gift. And, of course, the harder I tried to reach for it, the more elusive it became. It is there, as my pulse and breath are there. It is a part of ME. The only thing that may block its flow is my mind. Fear and uncertainty are the walls in this world of intent and belief. Doing instead of being interferes with the process.

As the doubts grew, I feared I was losing myself and so I might have."

The Reiki Cleanse

When a person receives a Reiki attunement, besides opening her Reiki channels, the attunement causes her entire vibrational level to be raised. From that moment onward, her entire being is forever changed.

The new Reiki practitioner may experience various physical or emotional symptoms as her body adjusts to the change in her vibrational level. We call this period a Reiki cleanse. She may experience a cleansing through bowels or kidneys or even a runny nose, as toxins are released from her body. Symptoms of old physical ailments may flare up briefly and intensify for a few minutes or hours before they are permanently released from the new practitioner's energy field. Emotions may bubble up and be released before she can even determine where they came from. Old problems may show up and be resolved in dreams. It generally takes twenty-one days for this cleansing period to be complete.

Change in Vibrational Level

Besides the changes we experience within ourselves after the attunement process, the changes in our vibrational level affect the way we are perceived by others. People who never noticed us before may be drawn to us. People coming from a more negative place may find us uncomfortable to be around and tend to avoid us. They may even try to start arguments with us.

The day of her first Reiki attunement, Donna, a rather reserved woman, phoned me after she arrived home and said, "Jeri, the strangest thing just happened to me. I stopped at the bakery on the way home and everyone kept coming up and talking to me. A little old Mexican man even came up to chat with me and I don't speak Spanish. It's like they were all drawn to me. And then when I arrived home, I went to let my dog in from the back porch. At first she acted like she didn't even know who I was and she wouldn't come into the house. All of a sudden, her ears perked up when she recognized me. Then, as soon as she came into the house, she stuck her head under my hand and the Reiki started to flow. Now the dog won't leave me alone!"

My own experience the day after my master attunement had a similar flavor. I drove out to the barn to play with my horse. Shortly after my arrival, a young girl I had never seen before came up to me and started telling me all about her horse and 4H. She followed me around like a little puppy dog for the entire evening happily chattering away as though I were her oldest friend.

I saw the flip side of the coin when I returned to work. The one physician in the group with whom I had never gotten along very well suddenly found fault with everything I did and said. It was as if my very presence in a room sent prickles down his spine. For a long time, it was difficult for us to even be in the same room together.

When my friend Marsha was watching her daughter play soccer, a small child she had never met before came up to her and took her hand. The child placed Marsha's hand on top of her own head. The Reiki began to flow and the child continued to hold Marsha's hand on her head for several minutes as if she were filling up at a gas station. When the little one had enough, she dropped Marsha's hand, gave her a quick hug and then, replete, ran off to play.

One day as Marsha and her daughter were loading their car in a grocery store parking lot, an old woman came up and started telling Marsha about her medical problems. As she continued to speak, the old woman took both Marsha's hands in her own and held them to her face. The Reiki began to flow. The old woman continued to press Marsha's hands to her cheeks until she was finished talking. At the end of her monologue, she released my friend's hands and went on her way.

When Marsha returned to the car, her daughter asked, "Who was that old woman?"

Marsha shrugged her shoulders. There was a little smile on her face when she said, "I have no idea."

When my friend Patricia first learned Reiki, her husband expressed a lack of interest in receiving treatments in spite of the fact that he was always in pain because of crippling arthritis in his knee. His body must have been more willing than his conscious mind. Pat told me that whenever she gave herself Reiki treatments in bed at night, her sleeping husband would roll over, take one of her hands, and place it on his arthritic knee for treatment.

Teaching Traditions

In Dr Usui's time, a student spent several years with her teacher when she studied to become a Reiki practitioner. She would receive additional attunements to increase her abilities whenever her teacher felt she had learned enough and was ready to receive them.

In modern times, it has become increasingly more impractical for this type of student-teacher relationship to exist. To solve this problem, Mrs. Takata created a system that divided the teaching of Reiki into three levels. She would instruct her students in one level over the course of a few days. The students returned home and practiced what they had learned. If and when Mrs. Takata decided that a student was ready, that student was allowed to progress to the next level.

In her entire lifetime, Mrs. Takata only attuned twenty-one Reiki Masters. For many years only the Grand Master, Mrs. Takata, knew the attunements that allow others to attain the level of Reiki Master. She passed this information on only to her granddaughter. It was the granddaughter who eventually chose to pass on this knowledge to all the Reiki Masters she herself taught. It was the decision to pass on this knowledge that has allowed Reiki training to finally become available to much of the world.

Levels of Reiki Training

In first degree Reiki, the student's channels are opened to the Reiki. She is then able to use it to perform hands-on healings on herself and others.

After some months or years, if the student is to move on, she receives second degree training. After her second degree attunement, the practitioner's ability to channel energy is dramatically increased. With this attunement, the Reiki symbols are placed into the student's hands and she becomes capable of performing not only hands-on but also distance healings.

Those few practitioners who are truly dedicated to teaching the traditions of Reiki become Reiki Masters. Only a Reiki Master is empowered with the ability to attune another person so that she, too, may become a Reiki practioner.

And so, we continue the ancient traditions that were rediscovered by Dr. Usui as we bring Reiki into the modern world.

Jesus did not heal those he healed
because he saw their condition as imperfect.
He healed those souls asking for healing
as part of their process...
He did not perform a random healing.
To do so would have been to violate
a sacred law of Universe:
"Allow each soul to walk its path."
~ **Conversations With God**
by Neale Walsch

CHAPTER TWENTY

Not Ready for Self Healing

I used to believe that, as a Reiki practitioner, it should always be my goal to empower my clients with the ability to heal themselves. I knew that receiving a Reiki treatment from another person is a wonderful, nurturing experience. My friend Sarah's experiences with her mother had taught me that repeated treatments from someone else could not only suppress physical symptoms but also heal a relationship. I knew that a few sessions with another healer could release energy blocks that an individual may be unable to break through with self-healing. In spite of all this, I still felt that as long as my clients depended on me, the healer, to control the symptoms of chronic conditions and maintain their state of well-being, their healing would never be complete. I believed it was my sacred duty to empower them with the ability of self-healing.

When a friend of mine who is also a Reiki Master occasionally mentioned one of her long-term clients to me, I became angry with her. As much as I love receiving treatments and performing healings, I actually thought it was unethical for her to continue to have these people come to her week after week instead of giving them the ability and the power to heal themselves. It seemed to me that she was providing a crutch without ever giving them the ability to fly free.

Of course, Spirit sent a lesson to help me understand this issue.

I became friends with a woman whose mother was a favorite patient of mine. At some point my friend, MJ, developed a condition that caused her to have severe chronic back pain. After medical evaluation, she was told the condition was incurable. Her doctor referred her to a pain clinic where the anesthesiologist wanted to give her epidural injections of a local anesthetic every six weeks or so for the rest of her life to control the pain. I was horrified.

I suggested that before she start letting people stick needles into her spine, she should come over for a Reiki treatment to see if it would help. She came for the treatment and for a week after the first session, her pain was gone. We were both very excited. After her second treatment session, I loaned her a copy of *Empowerment Through Reiki* to read and suggested that she come to my next Reiki class. I wanted her to be able to treat herself, to control her own pain.

Two weeks later, she arrived at the class, book in hand. She told me she had been too busy to open the book. Three other people were scheduled to participate in that class but only two showed up. MJ immediately suggested that we postpone the class until the fourth person was free.

"Nonsense," I said. "The others have been looking forward to this class for months. I certainly won't change their plans because someone else has chosen not to be here."

And so the class began. I spent an hour or two discussing the history of Reiki and the attunement process and sharing other information that I always present at a first degree Reiki class. I led them through a short, guided meditation, and then we took a break before beginning the attunement process.

MJ came up to me looking extremely ill at ease. "I'm just not ready to learn Reiki right now," she told me. "Maybe after I quit smoking I can take on this extra burden." She left the class. The following week she began having epidural injections at the pain clinic.

What did I learn from all of this? First and foremost, I learned that just because I think Reiki is wonderful and can do anything you ask it to does not mean that it is the right path for everyone.

I also learned how essential it is to consider the needs of the individual in question. MJ worked full time. She was a single parent to a teen-aged daughter. "In her spare time," she was the primary caretaker for her elderly, debilitated parents. She took care of her whole world. At that moment in her life, she was not ready to take on the burden of treating her own physical problems as well. Perhaps she even needed her illness because it was the only thing that gave her permission, every once in a while, to have someone else take care of *her* for a change.

If I wouldn't provide her with treatments then she was willing to have a man stick needles into her back. She would do whatever it took to have someone else take care of her.

I never again felt it was my right to push someone into taking a Reiki class. It is not up to me to decide what is in someone else's best interest. I believe it's acceptable to tell people about Reiki and what it can do and to let them know that the class is available. I always finish this type of conversation by saying that Reiki is not for everyone. If someone thinks she would like to learn Reiki, I encourage her to read a basic Reiki book. I ask that *she* call *me* if she is still interested in learning after reading the book. I make it very clear that it's perfectly OK with me if she decides not to learn Reiki.

*A thousand obstacles stand between our selves
and the honoring of our truth*
~Journal Notes: The Quiet Entity
by Rod Mac Iver

CHAPTER TWENTY-ONE

Exchange of Energy

One of the Reiki precepts is that there should always be an exchange of energy for healing. Dr. Usui learned this lesson quite painfully when, after seven years of giving away healings in the beggars' quarter in Kyoto, he realized that many of the people he worked with had never really healed. They did not value or even particularly desire the gift they had received, ·so their healing was incomplete.

Intellectually, the importance of an exchange of energy made perfect sense to me. In spite of this, it took some personal lessons for me to fully understand the importance of putting the concept into practice. When I first began doing energy work, my confidence was low and I felt that I needed to practice for a while before asking for anything in return for healing sessions. I don't think there was anything wrong with that in the beginning. It could even be rationalized that there *was* an exchange of energy. I gave them Reiki and they gave me confidence in my abilities as a healer. There does, however, come a time when, in order to be an effective healer, the healer must put a value on her own work or no one else will value what she has to offer.

The first inkling that perhaps my need to constantly give Reiki away as a gift was not always the best way to do things came when I taught my first Reiki class.

When I stopped working at the hospital, I offered to teach a class free of charge as a goodbye present to the nurses I had worked with on labor wing. I limited the class to six students and put others off until a second class. Only three of the six showed up. The others never even called to cancel so someone else could take their place. Of the three women who did come, two took the class seriously. The third woman kept going outside to smoke cigarettes, acting as though she were only there for a social afternoon. That woman rarely used her Reiki after the class.

I did charge a small fee for subsequent classes, but I still couldn't bring myself to take money from my friends. With two exceptions, the friends I taught without requesting some form of exchange of energy do not use the Reiki and have little regard for it.

These events finally made me understand that if someone doesn't value Reiki enough to give something of value in exchange for learning, then they probably don't really want to learn at all.

By no means do I intend to imply that there must be an exchange of *money* when Reiki is taught. In my personal experience, the exchange of energy for Reiki classes has come in the form of pieces of pottery, a dream-catcher, crystals, riding lessons, and repairs to my home. The possibilities are endless. What is important is that both parties feel that what has been exchanged between them was of comparable value.

The time I felt most dearly compensated for teaching someone Reiki, there was no money exchanged at all. I was in Findhorn, Scotland, for a medical meeting and a Therapeutic Touch class. One of my classmates, Carrie, was a second degree Reiki practitioner. When I asked her if she planned to take a master class, she looked at me like she thought I was crazy. "I wish I could, but I could never afford the six thousand pounds that it costs to take a master class in Scotland!"

It distressed me to know that, in this world where healing energy is so desperately needed, the price of Reiki was so high in her country that only very few people could afford it. So while I was there, Carrie had a private class. She became Scotland's first nontraditional (less expensive) Reiki Master. I was still in my "it's OK to give it away stage", but Carrie understood the importance of an exchange of energy.

Carrie had attended her first and second degree Reiki classes with her mother whom she adored. During the second degree class, her mother gave her a large citrine crystal. Her mother had a heart attack and died two weeks after that class. After her master class, Carrie presented me with the crystal from her mother. I always felt I was overpaid for teaching Carrie. To this day, every time I teach a Reiki class, I carry that stone in my pocket.

I had finally learned the importance of requesting an exchange of energy for a class but it was still very difficult for me to ask for anything in return when I performed healings. Reaching out to relieve pain has always been as natural a reflex as breathing for me. Giving a Reiki treatment is such a joy that I felt the privilege of giving the treatment was payment enough I couldn't bring myself to request anything in return.

When I was at the hospital, my patients were paying for my care. I considered the Reiki I offered them to be part of the package. Spending a few minutes to fix owies for the nurses was a valuable way of educating the medical community to the possibilities of energy healing and so I felt completely justified giving away the treatments. I rationalized that offering first aid at the ranch was a way of meeting people and becoming a part of the community. It also had the added effect of creating a community where Reiki was commonplace. This all seemed like payment enough for me. As usual, Spirit finally slapped me in the face one day and let me know that I needed to place a value on the healings I performed if I expected anyone else to value them.

Initially it seemed to me that Reiki was appreciated at the ranch, but at some point the line was crossed. I think it was crossed, in part because my students and I were always so available and willing to help that people began to take us for granted. We asked for nothing in return because simply providing the healing was a sheer joy for us. People who paid dearly for a weekly massage routinely received Reiki for free. Unfortunately, the unlimited availability of Reiki gave some people the impression that our work was not very valuable. After a horse's pain had been relieved with a Reiki treatment, one owner said, "Well, I'll just have the masseuse come out tomorrow to make sure she's really OK."

When a healer from Canada came to visit me at the stable, he took a few minutes to speak with a woman whose horse had been having some vague lameness problems. After looking at the animal, he told the woman her horse was taking on her anxiety and charged her fifty dollars for the consultation. He also discussed some healing techniques with her that he thought might help her child release the memories of some old, unresolved traumas. These were techniques that he and I had learned from the same teacher, techniques that I had already used, quite successfully, with the same woman to help her work out some issues she had with her ex-husband. At the end of the session, he left to return home to Canada. I told the woman I would be happy to do the work with the child. Her response was, "But he's a healer, you only do Reiki."

At this point in class, one of my students usually asks, "Does this mean that I should charge my husband for a Reiki treatment?" My answer is an unequivocal "NO". The exchange of money is not required. There is a constant exchange of energy within a family. If your husband asks for an hour-long Reiki treatment every day, then perhaps there should be a bartering of chores or a trip to a favorite restaurant.

We are also taught that we should only treat those who seek our services. In this society, where most people have never heard of Reiki, I think it's quite acceptable to introduce the subject ourselves. If a friend is hurting, I think it's OK to explain what Reiki is and to offer a treatment. However, if the person says, "No thank you," then we must humbly back off and drop the subject.

No matter how enthusiastic we are with our gift, it is not appropriate to force it onto someone else. "Oh please, just let me try. I know I can help you," is a totally unacceptable response to "No, thank you." "The offer is always open if you change your mind," is a far more appropriate response. We must honor other people's beliefs and comfort level.

Another frequently asked question is, "Am I supposed to charge my neighbor after I offer to help her?"

My answer is, "No, not when you offered." In the future, if she starts asking for healing sessions on a regular basis, then it *is* important to explain that there should be an exchange of energy. This does not mean that you need to ask your friend for money. You may ask your friend to teach you to crochet, to help you in the garden, to bake you a cake, or to walk your dog. What is important is that you both feel that what is exchanged is of equal value.

One of my students took the letter but not the true spirit of the meaning of exchange of energy to heart and told her friends, "I'll give you a Reiki treatment but you have to pay me one dollar."

I was horrified. I asked this woman who routinely paid sixty dollars for a weekly massage if she truly believed that her Reiki treatments were only worth one dollar. What she did was more devaluing of Reiki than giving it away for free.

Not only Reiki, but all of life must be a series of exchanges of energy. This point was brought home to me rather dramatically when I attended a lecture given by a man who works as a grief counselor for the Tucson AIDS Project. John told a story about one of his clients that totally changed my life.

John's relationship with the client, Dave, began when Dave was critically ill and completely bedridden. Dave's sister was providing his care which included bathing, feeding, and diaper changes. One day the woman turned to John and said, "This is the worst thing that could ever happen to my brother. Dave has always been a man who would do anything to help other people, but he would never let anyone do things for him. Here he is now, lying here like a baby, completely dependent on me for his every physical need."

John concluded, "Dave's experience illustrates a basic truth of the universe. There must always be balance in life. We *must* learn to receive as well as to give. If we don't achieve balance in our own lives, then Spirit will create a situation where we are forced to accept what we would not take willingly."

This story struck me right in the heart. I have always been a caretaker. I never think twice about doing things for other people, but like Dave, asking for help is one of the hardest things in the world for me to do. Now, when I need help, I think of that story. I don't want to end up in a situation where Spirit will be forced to create balance for me, so I have learned to ask for help.

In closing this discussion, I would like to reiterate that requesting an exchange of energy for healing is not a polite way of turning a healing practice into a business. There is a strong universal principle at work here, one that Dr. Usui learned at great spiritual expense in the beggars' quarter in Kyoto. Dave learned it with his life. For healing to take place, there *must* be balance. The abilities of the healer mean little without desire of the client to be healed. The client must place enough value on the healing that she is willing to put something of herself into the process.

CHAPTER TWENTY-TWO

Healing Sessions

Reiki Hand Positions

A healing or a Reiki treatment may be as simple or as complex as the practitioner deems necessary. Almost every Reiki book I've read contains drawings that illustrate a set of "traditional" hand positions for Reiki treatments. I have met a number of practitioners who believe that the most important thing for a Reiki healer to know is exactly where to place her hands when giving a treatment. It troubles me to see people so focused on these trivial details that they fail to grasp the essence of Reiki and energy medicine.

Before discussing the treatment session itself, let's step back for a moment and take a look at the history and evolution of the Reiki hand positions to see if we can't put their importance into a little better perspective.

We have been told that when Dr. Usui performed a healing, he placed his hand on a single pulse point on the healee's body and simply allowed the Reiki to flow until the healing was complete. Dr. Hayashi later developed a series of four hand positions that his healing teams used when they performed healings. It was not until the third generation of modern Reiki Masters, when Reiki was brought to America, that Mrs. Takata created what are now referred to as the "traditional Reiki hand positions".

Stories relate that Mrs. Takata taught these hand positions in a different order to different students. Some of her students were taught to begin treatments at the client's head, some were told to begin at the client's feet. Still others were instructed to begin their treatments at the heart chakra. I think we can conclude from this brief history that there is no strict dogma associated with the hand positions and that they are not the essence of Reiki. The hand positions are merely guidelines for treatment sessions.

I believe the Reiki hand positions are most important for new Reiki practitioners. When a person first steps into the world of energy medicine, she must develop a totally different understanding of healing than the average Westerner has grown up with.

Western society has turned healing into medicine and medicine into a very sophisticated job of plumbing. The leap from swallowing pills, sewing lacerations, and nailing together broken bones, to following one's intuition and dancing in the human energy field can be an incomprehensible one for many Westerners. The "traditional hand positions" create a concrete structure and form for a healing session. They make the more abstract concepts of Eastern healing methods seem a little less etheric, so they become easier to assimilate for the newly initiated Westerner.

The hand positions also serve several other purposes. They give the inexperienced healer a specific job to do so she doesn't need to worry about whether or not she is intuitive enough to perform a healing. They guide her to treat the client's entire body and give someone unaccustomed to touching a stranger for healing, permission to touch. Repetition of the "standard treatment" provides an arena in which the practitioner will gradually develop the ability to sense subtle changes in her clients' energy fields and will gain confidence in her abilities as a healer.

Self-Healing
The ability to perform self-healings is one of the major factors that sets Reiki apart from other healing systems. Reiki isn't only about reaching out to other people, it's about empowering ourselves, taking control of our own healing, and honoring ourselves.

In class, before I pass the first attunement, I always ask my students to raise their right hand and promise that, for at least the duration of the twenty-one day cleanse, they will give themselves a full Reiki treatment each day. I encourage them to set aside at least an hour for this purpose, even if it has to be in the middle of the night. This hour should be a time when they think of no one but themselves and their own healing.

When we review the traditional hand positions for self-healing, I suggest they begin some of their self-healing sessions at their heads and other sessions at their feet. I like them to do this because they often become so relaxed after Reiki flows through their heads that they fall asleep and never treat the rest of their bodies. Starting the occasional treatment at their feet assures that each chakra receives attention at least some of the time.

There is a classic energy cycle that occurs when a Reiki practioner places her hands for healing. The palms of the healer become very warm as Reiki begins to flow. When an area has drawn all the Reiki it needs at the moment, the flow of energy stops and the healer's hands cool down again. The cooling of her hands is the signal to move them to a new position. The cycle usually takes about five minutes for a first degree practitioner. However, if one chakra needs a lot of healing, it may draw energy for an hour or more or for as long as the practitioner leaves her hands in that location.

The new Reiki practitioner may not immediately perceive the changes that occur in her hands when energy flows. This is why I suggest that my students give themselves their first few treatments by the clock, changing hand positions every three to five minutes. Having such concrete guidelines alleviates the tendency to focus their concentration on physical sensations that are new and foreign to them. It prevents them from spending the entire session trying to analyze each sensation and worrying about whether they are "doing it right". With experience comes confidence. Soon the new practitioner will sense what is happening during a healing without having to consciously evaluate each action.

Ideally, a Reiki practitioner should give herself a full treatment every day. She deserves to be able to nurture herself in this way. Sadly, contemporary life styles do not always allow for this much time on a daily basis. This doesn't mean that there is no time for Reiki. You don't have to concentrate on what you're doing to give yourself Reiki. You don't even need to use two hands. You just have to lay down your hands with the intent that the Reiki will flow. Once the process has turned itself on, you can direct your attention elsewhere.

When I read, watch TV, or talk on the phone, I give myself Reiki. While driving in light traffic, I keep one hand on the wheel, place the other on my heart and give myself Reiki. I used to walk around hospital corridors with one hand on my solar plexus and one on my second chakra. I was occasionally asked if I had a stomach ache, but no one ever thought I was crazy. This practice assured that I always had time to give myself Reiki, even when I was working 120 hours a week!

Treating Another Person

Before beginning a Reiki treatment, I explain to the person about to receive the healing that she may feel warmth, tingling, or pressure where the Reiki is flowing or she may feel nothing at all. After reassuring her that nothing I do should cause her pain or discomfort, I request that she inform me immediately should any pain begin or intensify during the course of the treatment. Occasionally, there is a brief period when a pain is intensified as a physical injury begins to heal. If I know this is happening, I can redirect the treatment or even scoop the pain away with my hands. Reiki is NOT like massage. "No pain, no gain" is NOT the message of the day.

I tell my client she is free to talk if she feels like it, explaining that I will always respond to her but that I generally won't start a conversation. I don't want my chatting to interfere with her healing process if she is deep in thought. I reassure her that it's also OK if she goes to sleep.

Clearing yourself

Before laying my hands on another person for healing, I take a moment to clear and center myself. While taking a slow deep breath, I draw healing energy into my crown chakra. On the exhale, I drive the energy along with any negative emotions I may have been carrying through my body, out of my feet, and into the earth. I then take a second to visualize and reinforce the silver protective bubble that surrounds and protects me. (see Chapter 16)

Scanning

I like to scan the person's energy field to get a sense of trouble spots and energy blocks at the beginning of a treatment. To do this I hold my hands about four inches above my client, placing the heel of my right hand in front of the tips of the fingers of my left hand. This position allows me to evaluate differences between the left and the right sides of my client's energy field. Beginning with my hands at the level of her crown chakra, I quickly and smoothly pass my hands over the length of her energy field ending at the level of her feet.

It is important to move quickly and fluidly in order to sense what is present in her energy field. Hesitations in the movement allow time for the healer's Reiki to begin interacting with and changing the client's energy field. This makes it difficult to tell what the condition of the client's aura really is. If I perceive a lot of inconsistencies in a client's energy field, I often use the sweeping motions of Therapeutic Touch (see chapter 25) to begin to gently shift energy blocks before starting my Reiki treatment.

If a client has never before experienced energy work and is a little uncertain of the process, I may not scan her energy field at the beginning of a session. My primary goal is to make my client comfortable. If the concept of energy work is foreign to someone, beginning a treatment by waving my hands about in the air above her body may make her so uneasy that she'll be unable to relax and enjoy the treatment.

Scanning can be a frustrating prospect for the new practitioner. I constantly remind my students that they are learning to collect and interpret a form of information that is completely new and foreign to them. Their brains will need time to learn how to process this information.

When a child first learns to walk, the movements and sensations are unfamiliar to her. The smallest step requires a major effort. Eventually, the connections are made between feet and brain, and walking becomes as natural to the child as breathing.

I explain to my students that the first time they scan someone's energy field, the action may be just as difficult for them as learning to walk. The more frequently they repeat the process, the quicker the connections will be made between hands and brain. When this happens, the information will become available to them when they scan someone's energy field.

It is also important for people to understand that when they do healing work, their dominant sense may not be touch. I am extremely kinesthetic so when I run my hands through a human energy field, I feel thin and dense and hot and cold places. When my friend Lisa, whose dominant healing sense is sight, runs her hands through the same energy field, she sees red or green or blue or black. The nerves in her hands receive the same information mine did, but the information is interpreted differently by her brain. My brain reads texture and temperature, hers sees color. Some healers may hear certain sounds when they scan an energy field, others may perceive various odors which tell them what's going on. As we become more experienced healers, each of us must learn to gather information from any and all of our senses.

The Treatment

After scanning the client's energy field, I encourage my students to proceed with the traditional Reiki hand positions. Should they feel strongly drawn to break from the traditional order and place their hands at some specific location, I advise them to honor their intuition.

One should never have to work to make Reiki flow. My own teacher likened the Reiki practioner to a golden funnel connecting the universal Reiki source to the client. After having received the proper attunements, all the healer has to do to give Reiki is to place her hands on a person and get out of the way. The healer is only a funnel. It is the choice of the client whether or not she will remove the stopper from the end of the funnel and allow Reiki to flow into her body, mind, and spirit.

When Reiki is flowing, the practitioner's palms usually become very hot. At times, the practitioner will be aware of the sensation of heat coming from her hands. She may also feel a tingling sensation or a kind of pressure like the feeling experienced when holding two magnets together. The inexperienced practitioner may perceive none of this.

The person receiving the healing may feel warmth, pressure, tingling, or just soft hands. The conscious perceptions of the healer and the client do not necessarily correlate with each other or with the flow of energy. If a new practitioner constantly tries to analyze the sensations in her hands, she may actually sabotage herself with the worry she is generating and block the flow of energy.

When I gave Reiki treatments to my labor patients, I couldn't always feel the Reiki flowing from my hands into the patient's uterus. At these times, my patient often told me how warm my hands were on her belly. Sometimes, she would sleep through her contractions as I watched them being recorded on the uterine monitor. The lesson in all this is to just let it happen. It is not beneficial to constantly analyze the process. Just put your hands down, ask the Reiki to flow, and see what happens.

When a student is uncertain of what she is feeling, her tendency is often to press harder. My recommendation is, "If you're unsure, lighten up." Reiki can reach someone when it is sent from a thousand miles away. There is certainly no need to shove your hands painfully into someone's flesh to reach tissues that are only inches away.

At times, it can be helpful for students to raise their hands up into the client's etheric field for part of a session. When the familiar physical sensations of cloth and body are removed, it becomes easier for the healer to perceive the movement of energy and this can be reassuring to students. Still, I repeatedly tell my students the Reiki will flow whether they feel it or not. I try to convince them to leave their analytical minds in the other room. The best thing they can do is to become a golden funnel and let their conscious mind get out of the way.

Body Mechanics

A Reiki practitioner never needs to worry about her own energy being depleted when she gives a treatment. She is only a vessel through which universal life force energy is free to pass. There is an unlimited abundance of Reiki in the universe. When the energy passes through a Reiki practitioner, her body will absorb as much energy as she needs without interrupting the flow to her client. This means that the Reiki practitioner actually receives a treatment every time she administers one.

In spite of this, the physical act of performing a healing can be tiring if the practitioner does not use her body properly. The healer should assume the most comfortable position that circumstances permit. She should attempt to position her arms in a way that will be effective without causing undue strain on her own muscles. One way to do this is to rest her upper arms on her torso and to extend only the lower half of the arm whenever this will allow for adequate reach. Another is to adjust a stool or table to a height that is most comfortable for the healer.

Intuition

Starting a treatment at a client's head has several benefits. If a person is unaccustomed to being touched, a hand placed gently on her head is a nonthreatening way to establish physical contact. This gives the client a chance to begin to feel safe in the healer's hands. Receiving Reiki energy around the head also helps the client to relax and puts her into a more receptive state for the rest of the healing.

If a client has an abuse history, she may only tolerate being touched on her head or feet. When enough healing has occurred, she will begin to feel safe and allow other parts of her body to be touched during a treatment. Using the full compliment of hand positions may, at times, facilitate the process for the healer, however anything that interferes with the emotional or physical comfort of the client is counterproductive. We must always keep in mind the basic principle that as long as the energy is made available, the Reiki will go where it needs to go.

As a healer becomes more experienced and her intuitive abilities become more refined, her understanding of the specific needs of her client will tend to direct the pattern of a healing. During the course of a treatment session, the healer may feel compelled to place her hands at some particular location where the energy will proceed to flow for a long time. On some occasions, she may be drawn to spend a lot of time balancing the energy between chakras or removing blocks from specific areas. It is not unusual for a healer to hear comments from her clients like, "That's exactly where it hurts. How did you know?"

Dealing With Energy Blocks

If an energy block is present, I *could* simply place my hands over it and let the Reiki flow until the block dissolves. Done in this way, my client might experience pressure, pain, or even a choking sensation in the blocked chakra as it is bombarded with Reiki. I am *not* of the "no pain, no gain" school. When I encounter a situation where the direct flow of energy creates either physical or emotional discomfort for my client, I resort to various other methods for removing the energy block. This eliminates my client's discomfort without sacrificing the effectiveness of the treatment.

When I encounter an energy block, one of the first things I do is to use Therapeutic Touch techniques. Beginning with my hands in the same position I use for scanning, I repeatedly brush my hands across her energy field moving from head to feet. I use my hands and my intent to gently free up any accumulations of dense, negative energy and "smooth out" the client's energy field.

If that doesn't solve the problem, I try to remove the energy block by gathering the negative energy into my hands and throwing it away. The motion resembles the act of scooping up a pile of cookie crumbs from the top of a table. Once the negative energy has been gathered up in my hands, I form it into a ball. Holding the energy ball in one hand, I use the other hand to cut it loose from my client's body. With my hands and my intent, I throw the energy ball away into a cosmic garbage can. This is a conduit I visualize whose purpose is to direct the ball of negative energy into the center of the earth where it can be recycled into positive energy.

For more resistant energy blocks, a stone or crystal can be useful. I often choose a piece of rose quartz. After laying the stone over the energy block, I run Reiki through it. The negative energy collects in the stone as the block is released. The stone frequently becomes very dull or even changes color as this process occurs. After removing the stone, it should immediately be placed into a salt water bath to neutralize the negative energy and clean the stone.

These methods are gentle, painless, and effective ways to break through energy blocks. My patients may have had pain from surgery or when delivering their babies, but there is absolutely no reason to cause them pain or discomfort with Reiki.

Setting

I like to darken the room and play soft music when performing a healing. The music helps both me and my client to relax. While listening to the music, I often let my consciousness drift away from my body. I stay aware enough of the sensations in my body to know when to move my hands. If I need to respond to a client's conversation, I bring my consciousness fully back into my body. At times, I go into a mode of deep concentration in order to focus my intent to remove a block or to fix some internal damage I feel can be dealt with more efficiently by using some other healing techniques.

I think a newly trained practitioner is probably best listening to music, chatting, or even reciting the multiplication tables. These activities will prevent her from worrying about what is happening in her hands.

Completing a Session

At the end of a healing session, I generally scan my client's energy field again to be sure there are no major blocks or hot spots still present. To me, someone's energy field should feel smooth at the end of a session. If there are minor inconsistencies in her aura, I smooth them out with a little Therapeutic Touch. If that doesn't do the trick, I keep working. A healing should not end when a bell rings, it should end when the work is finished.

Ethics

Giving a Reiki treatment is an extremely warm and loving experience for both healer and client. It is the act of channeling pure love from the universe into another person. It's important to understand that the loving feelings are part of the Reiki treatment and not the beginnings of a more intimate relationship. When someone seems particularly enchanted with me during a Reiki treatment, I often suggest that they reach up and touch the back of my hands. The totally average feel of the back of my hands is such a dramatic contrast to the almost magical feeling of the Reiki flowing from my palms that this simple demonstration usually serves to gently release any inappropriate attachment my client is beginning to form for me.

At the end of a treatment, I use the ritual of washing my hands to symbolize the act of separating myself from my client. An old friend of mine used to face his client at the end of each treatment session and say out loud, " I respectfully return to you any of your energy that I may have picked up during this session and I respectfully request that you return any of my energy back to me."

Mini-Treatments

After discussing full treatments, I think it's important to add another reminder that a little Reiki is better than none at all. However nice it may be to have a full hour, a special healing room, and a message table, these things are not essential to give a Reiki treatment.

A five minute Reiki session while she sat in a chair in the office helped our head nurse to relax before she had to face an unpleasant meeting with management. A brief treatment on a picnic bench at the stables helped my friend Jennifer forget her fears and relax before her first horse show. She won her class.

Though a bale of hay or a picnic table may be less comfortable than a massage table, the healing will be no less valuable. The only thing that is necessary to give a Reiki treatment is a practioner who has received the proper attunements and a body that desires to receive the energy. There are no rules or regulations that make a Reiki treatment correct or incorrect. As long as there is a pure intent to heal, the energy will flow and the healing will be done.

CHAPTER TWENTY-THREE

Healing Acute
and
Chronic Conditions

The treatment for acute conditions tends to be different from the treatment for chronic conditions in Western medicine. The same is also true in energy medicine.

When dealing with an acute problem like a tension headache, the pain from a recent surgical incision or labor pain, a single energy treatment will usually suffice to relieve the pain and accelerate the healing process.

At times, chronic pain may result from an acute insult. For example, the phantom pain experienced by an amputee results from a single incident where energy pathways were severed as diseased flesh was cut away from the body. This type of chronic pain may be relieved with a single treatment. When Reiki is used to re-establish old energy pathways that were severed during the operation, the pain will often be permanently relieved.

Chronic illness resulting from a long-standing condition like liver disease, heart failure, arthritis, or depression will benefit from energy therapy. One must realize, however, that a condition that has evolved gradually over months or years will rarely be cured with a single treatment. In these instances, repeated treatments will often result in dramatic improvement.

I have seen Reiki cause enormous improvement in children with ADHD and Tourette's syndrome, in people with chronic depression, and in people with the pain of fibromyalgia and chronic arthritis. In my own experience, symptoms may be relieved for one to three days after a single treatment. Does the recurrence of symptoms signify that the Reiki is an inadequate treatment? Absolutely not. All these conditions, if treated with Western medicine, would require the life-long administration of drugs. These drugs often have the potential for causing side effects that can be as debilitating as the primary disease. If I am able to relieve someone's symptoms equally well with an occasional energy treatment, I consider this a success.

I believe the best long-term solution to treating chronic conditions is for the client to learn Reiki herself. By doing so, she may eventually become completely independent of me and fully responsible for her own healing.

In many ways, energy work is ultimately more effective than medication. Medicines relieve symptoms. Energy work treats the mental, emotional, and spiritual condition that is at the root of chronic disease. The ability to perform self-healing empowers the chronically ill individual who often feels like the victim of her disease. It gives her back control of her own life.

No matter how gifted the healer, it would be irresponsible and dangerous to abruptly discontinue all Western medical treatment and switch to pure energy medicine. It is not unusual, however, for people with chronic illnesses to eventually be able to be weaned off many medications as the disease process is gradually reversed. This weaning should always be done under a doctor's supervision.

Not all people are willing to commit the time and effort needed to bring about their own healing. I am constantly amazed when people who expect to take a handful of pills every day for the rest of their lives feel that a single hour of energy work should bring about a complete cure. If they are not cured in an hour, they dismiss energy medicine as useless.

One of my patients who has suffered from chronic depression and the constant pain of fibromyalgia for years, came to me one day for a Reiki treatment When she left my office, she was pain free and her depression had lifted. Her face was relaxed and glowing with a radiance I had never before seen in this woman. She made another appointment for the following week which she subsequently cancelled.

The next time I saw her, I asked why she had decided not to have the second Reiki treatment. "I felt wonderful when I left your office," she told me. "Actually, I don't remember when I last felt so good, but the effects of the treatment only stayed with me for a day or two. When my symptoms returned, I decided it was less trouble to simply take pills than to come for treatments or take a class."

As I've said before, not everyone is ready to make a commitment to healing and Reiki is not for everyone. I acknowledged her response and changed the subject.

The antithesis to this woman is my friend Miranda and her family. Miranda's two young sons had both recently been diagnosed with ADHD and Tourette's Syndrome, a neurologic disease that causes the afflicted person to experience involuntary physical movements and involuntary vocalizations. She was searching for anything that might help her children's conditions. She despised the idea of filling the boys full of drugs for the rest of their lives. A mutual friend told Miranda about her own experience with Reiki and referred her to me, hoping I might be able to help.

Miranda and her eleven-year-old son Michael arrived at my home on the appointed day. The boy played with my new puppy for a half hour or so while I sat by observing and chatting with his mother. There was a tremendous tension in all of Michael's movements as he and the puppy romped around the room together. The child constantly shifted positions creating the impression that he simply couldn't get comfortable in his own body. He never once became easy or relaxed as he played with the little dog.

When the child had been in the house long enough to become more at ease with me, we proceeded to my healing room. I worked on Michael for about half an hour. At the end of his treatment, we returned to the living room and the puppy.

Miranda and I both observed that, though he was still an active little boy, Michael seemed to be more relaxed and more comfortable with himself than he had been before the treatment. The urgency had left him.

The acid test came when Miranda and her son returned to her mother's house where they were spending the summer.

Miranda's parents had been appalled when she told them of her plan to bring the boy to me. They told her she was being foolish, wasting her time and money. After his Reiki treatment, even Miranda's parents acknowledged the difference in the child's behavior. That difference lasted for almost three days.

Miranda attended my next Reiki class. She wanted to be able to help the boys herself .

One of my greatest joys as a teacher is finding a student who loves Reiki as much as I do and who embraces it completely into her life. Those are the moments when I know my time and effort have been well spent. Miranda was one of those students.

She used Reiki every day on herself and on her children. The eleven-year-old was sometimes impatient of the process but seven- year-old Jessie loved Reiki and asked if he might learn too. His mother brought him to the house to receive a Reiki attunement.

Miranda continued to use Reiki every day. She gave the boys treatments at night when they slept. She used Reiki to fix the owies that frequently occured in a household of young boys. It helped everything from simple sunburn to the neurologic condition that afflicted both children.

To this day, Jessie has never received medication for the Tourettes Syndrome. Michael soon required less medication than his physicians anticipated. He is now off all medication as well. Miranda was able to stop home schooling and send her children to school where they both do well.

As a result of the long-term use of Reiki, the boys are free of medications and their many side effects. They live normal lives in spite of their affliction with Tourette's syndrome. Miranda herself is one of the most peaceful, loving individuals I have ever encountered. Undoubtedly, Miranda's story represents one of my most gratifying experiences as a Reiki practitioner and a teacher.

CHAPTER TWENTY-FOUR

Distance Healing

Second degree Reiki increases the scope of the Reiki practitioner's healing abilities in two ways. The second degree attunement raises her vibrational level and this dramatically increases her ability to channel Reiki energy. It's like transforming a gentle stream into a raging river. The second degree attunement also places the Reiki symbols into the practitioner's hands. The symbols can be used to direct the focus of a healing to mental and emotional planes. They also give the practitioner the means to transcend the barrier of space and time to perform distance healing.

The Reiki symbols can only be used by someone who has received the appropriate attunements from a Reiki Master. Traditionally, the student receives the symbols, which are considered to be sacred, in her second degree class. I will discuss the use of the symbols in order to explain the depth and the scope of Reiki, but, in honor of the ancient traditions, I have chosen not to include the Sanskrit names or the images of the symbols in this book. If you become a Reiki practitioner, your teacher will give you the names and images of the symbols at the appropriate time.

The Power Symbol

This symbol increases the power of any healing session and increases the power of the other symbols. The Power Symbol can be used to protect a room, to charge crystals, and to enrich the nutritional value of food and drink by filling them with Reiki. The symbol has been used to release trauma from the victim of an accident or injury. It has been used as a benediction.

When invoking the Power Symbol, I visualize it in its three dimensional form. I see the symbol as a funnel or energy vortex collecting healing energy from the Reiki source and channeling its flow directly into where ever I have placed the symbol.

The Emotional Symbol

The name of this symbol means "I have the key" (to the unconsciousness). The Emotional Symbol is used to direct healing toward the emotional aspects of disease. It facilitates the release of stored negative feelings and emotions such as fear, pain and anger. Left unresolved, these emotions ultimately manifest as physical or psychiatric disease.

The symbol can also be used to clear negative energy from a room or object and to release spirit attachments. When invoking this symbol, I visualize a dragon being sent out to devour negative emotions and memories.

The Distance Symbol

The name of this symbol means, "No past, no present, no future." This symbol is the key that unlocks the door to other dimensions. It erases the barriers between time and space, allowing us to direct healing energy to distant physical locations. It also enables us to direct healing to past or future events. The Distance Symbol facilitates karmic healing by granting the healer entrance into the Akashic records.

Clearing a Room With Reiki

The Reiki symbols can be used to clear a room to create a sacred space. As with most cleansing rituals, the four electromagnetic directions of the earth are addressed when using Reiki to cleanse and bless a room.

While facing toward the South, draw the Emotional Symbol in the air in front of yourself and say its name three times. Use your hands and your intent to throw the symbol into the wall in front of you. *See* the symbol filling the wall and the corners of the room. Turn ninety degrees to face the West and repeat the process. Send the Emotional Symbol to the walls in each of the four directions. Finally, return to face the direction where you began and say, "May this room be cleared of all negative energies and entities."

Send the distance symbol to all four directions in the

same manner and then say, "May the healing in this room transcend time and space."

Send the Power Symbol to all four directions and then say, "May this room be filled with the Reiki light."

During a Hands-on Healing

The Reiki symbols may be employed during a hands-on healing session to direct the focus of the healing. The Power Symbol may be used at any time to increase the intensity of the energy being channeled. If a client is trying to deal with an emotional issue, the Emotional Symbol may be invoked to facilitate the process. When an energy block is encountered, using the Distance Symbol directs the energy to past issues and will often break through the block.

Physical Healing at a Distance

In its most simplistic form, distance healing provides the means to perform the equivalent of a hands-on Reiki treatment on someone who is at a different physical location from the healer. When performing a distance healing, the healer must first obtain the consent of the recipient just as she should obtain permission for hands-on work.

It is a good idea to arrange the time when a distance healing is to take place. A person can become as relaxed while receiving a distance healing as she becomes during a hands-on healing session. It would be inadvisable to perform a distance healing when the recipient is at a business meeting, driving on the freeway or engaged in any other activity that requires her undivided attention.

Sending Distance Healing

Generally some physical object is used as the focus for a distance healing. It may be a doll that is meant to represent the person receiving the healing. It may be a piece of paper on which the healer has written the name of the person receiving the healing or a photograph of that person. It may be a written list of events the healer would like to manifest.

To send distance healing, first pick up the object you have chosen to be your focus for the healing. Repeat your intent three times either silently or aloud. Then hold the object in one hand while you use the other to write the Reiki symbols on the object or in the air above it. They should be written in the following order: Distance Symbol, Power Symbol, Emotional Symbol, Power Symbol. Whenever you invoke a symbol, repeat its name three times as you draw or visualize it. If you are alone, say the names aloud. If you are with other people or performing a hands-on healing, repeat the names in your mind.

Now, clasp the object between both hands. Again, visualize the symbols over the object and either state the intent to yourself or visualize a motion picture of what would be the result of that intent while the Reiki flows from your palms, through the object. If you are asking for the good health of a person or animal, visualize that person or animal performing activities that could only be performed in a healthy state. For example, when sending energy for an injured horse, I visualize the animal cantering effortlessly through a grassy field.

While continuing to send distance healing, I periodically blow the combination of symbols, or the Power Symbol alone, over my hands. Alternatively, I may beam them with my third eye or simply visualize the symbols above my hands. This increases the power of the healing. It's like repeatedly stepping on the gas pedal when you are driving a car.

Common Distance Healing Techniques

1.) Use a teddy bear as a surrogate for the client. After invoking the Distance, Power, Emotional and Power Symbols, give the bear a Reiki treatment with the intent that the energy be transferred to the person who has requested the healing.

2.) Invoke the symbols and send healing through a photograph of the recipient.

3.) Hold a crystal or other talisman and imagine that it represents the entire body of the recipient. Invoke the symbols and send energy through the crystal.

. 4.) Imagine that the recipient is in front of you. After invoking the Reiki symbols, visualize the recipient, raise your hands, and perform a healing as if the other person were actually there.

The fourth method is my favorite way to perform distance healing when focusing on a specific physical problem such as a headache. It is not an ideal method for performing the distance version of a full body healing because it can be physically exhausting to hold one's hand in the air for such an extended period of time.

When my Aunt Lois came from Columbus, Ohio, to visit me in Tucson, it goes without saying that I offered to give her a Reiki treatment. She loved it.

Some weeks later, while we were talking on the phone, she told me she had a terrible pain in her left arm. I said I'd try to make it go away if she wanted me to. "Sure," she replied.

As we continued to chat, I visualized Aunt Lois sitting in the room, right in front of me. I wrote the distance symbols in the air and then began a Reiki session as if her arm were in my hands. I could actually *feel* the energy field of her arm between my hands. The Reiki continued to flow as we proceeded with our conversation.

After a few minutes she abruptly changed the subject and said, "I can feel my arm tingling." I told her I was doing Reiki for her just as I had when she was at my house.

The rest of our conversation was interspersed with comments from my aunt like, "It's in my fingers now," and, "It's easing off." After a few minutes, she told me the pain was gone. We ended our conversation as if nothing unusual had happened.

A few weeks later when I was speaking with my little eighty- year- old aunt on the phone again, she told me she had recently been to see her doctor. She said that while she was there, she told him about the treatment I had given her during our last telephone conversation.

"Jeri," she said, "My doctor says Reiki must be some form of hypnosis, otherwise you could never have done it over the phone."

I just smiled.

On another occasion I was on the telephone with my friend Brent a few hours after he returned home from a dental appointment. When he told me he was experiencing a lot of pain, I offered to send him healing which he accepted.

As we continued our conversation, I imagined Brent's face in the air in front of me. After drawing the Reiki symbols over the image of his face, I lifted my hands and felt his energy field between them as if he were really in the room with me. We continued our conversation as I gave him a Reiki treatment He occasionally guided my hands with comments like, "A little to the left" and "The pain is focusing at the angle of my jaw, can you pull it off? Ah... That's better now." By the time we finished our conversation, his pain was gone.

Storing Reiki in a Healing Talisman

It is possible to fill an object with Reiki and set the intent so the recipient of the object can draw healing from it whenever she feels the need. For a small Child, one might choose a stuffed teddy bear. The bear is given to a child with the explanation that if she is sad or hurt or lonely, she may draw Reiki from her bear.

A crystal or other object may be programmed to serve the same purpose for an adult. Ethics demand that the healer explain the purpose of the Reiki-filled talisman to the recipient.

Cutting Psychic Cords

When a relationship has ended, the people involved often have a hard time letting go of the past and moving on with their lives. One reason for this is that one or both parties may still be holding on to the other person via a psychic cord. These cords are bands of energy that are formed by unresolved emotions. As long as they exist, it is impossible for either party to be completely free of the other. The connection prevents both people from becoming fully immersed in new relationships. To remove the cords, simply invoke the distance symbols and request that any cords or attachments that still exist between the two people be severed.

Healing Distant Times

While it is certainly nice to be able to send a Reiki treatment to someone in another location, I believe the greatest power of distance healing comes from the ability it gives the healer to transcend time.

Healing The Past

Being able to heal the past means we can go back to childhood or to past lives and heal situations that, left unresolved, have manifested as fear, disease, depression, insecurity, self-esteem issues, and other problems that affect us in the present time. One way to heal specific periods of our present life is by sending healing energy and positive affirmations through photographs of ourselves at various ages.

 In spite of two doctorates and a life filled with what outsiders thought to be considerable achievement, for many years I felt like a failure. Many of my insecurities stemmed from the fact that no matter how much I accomplished, my mother never once told me she was proud of me.

Distance healing changed the way I perceived myself. After collecting a group of pictures of my self at ages ranging from eighteen months to the present, I gathered the photos in my hands, invoked the Reiki symbols, and began to send energy. While the energy poured through my palms, I visualized the baby picture. I spoke to the little baby Jeri. I told her over and over again, "I love you, baby. You're a sweet little girl, and I'm proud of you." Next, I focused my intent on the eight-year- old version of myself and told her, "I love you, Jeri. You're a beautiful, talented little girl. I'm proud of you, and I'll never send you away." I progressed through all the photos ending the session with the most recent photos of myself as an adult.

After that session, for the first time in my life, I was able to say out loud, "I'm proud of myself" and mean it. The sad little girl trying so desperately to please her mother finally matured. She became the woman of power who had always been buried deep inside of me.

Healing Trauma

Many therapies geared towards healing the affects of past trauma require that the victim mentally revisit the trauma as part of the process. With Reiki distance healing, it is possible to go back to the time before the incident and heal the situation that led up to the trauma and essentially rewrite the past without forcing the client to relive a painful situation. This process removes the effects the trauma would have had on the future and heals the victim's spirit.

It is possible to use distance healing during a hands-on healing session. A woman is afraid to leave her home after dark because she was once assaulted while taking a walk in the evening. The healer invokes the distance symbols as she asks the client to picture herself on the night of the assault and to imagine what might have happened if, instead of turning left when she left her driveway, as she did the night of the assault, she had chosen to turn right. The client is guided to visualize herself walking around the block and returning safely to her home.

The use of the distance symbols actually takes the client back in time so she can relive the event with the more positive outcome. The memory of the trauma is replaced by the memory of an uneventful walk, and the fear can be released.

When performing only a distance session for the same client, the Reiki practitioner may simply send healing to the event that was the cause of her client's fears.

Healing Relationships

When healing a relationship, it is important to send energy in a way that is free from anger or blame. One might send healing while stating, "I wish to send energy to the event that was the origin of the Karma between myself and ___." or "I wish to send healing to all situations in all lifetimes where ___ and I encountered each other's spirits."

Healing the Future: Manifestation

Future healing can be as simple as sending energy to yourself at a specified time the following day when you expect to be busy and tired.

Distance healing can also be sent to affect a future situation. This is when the ethics of Reiki are most important. You may ask for anything, but you must *not* ask in such a way that your gain will cause harm or loss to someone else. Reiki will never harm another person but you *can* create negative karma for yourself by attempting to send energy that could be harmful to someone else.

The night before a meeting between my neighbors and some people from the next subdivision who were disputing our right to use a certain access road, I sent energy in the following way, "I ask that the spirit of anger be absent from tomorrow's meeting. I ask that a solution be found that is fair and just for all parties concerned."

When asking for something to manifest, be specific. A careless request can undermine your own intent. In other words, "Be careful what you ask for, you may get it."

Jane, a vivacious forty-five year old, laughingly recalled the results of some of her own distance healing sessions. "Each time I sent energy, I included a request that a man who was warm, sensitive, kind, honest, and caring come into my life. I just met the man I was describing. Unfortunately, he's eighty-five. When sending the energy, I was hoping to meet my life partner, but it never occurred to me to specify age. Oh well... I did get what I was asking for, I just wasn't specific enough, and I've found a wonderful friend!"

When sending manifestation energy for someone else, you must *never* try to control their lives with your desires. To do so is against the ethics of Reiki and against the laws of universe. Even though there is absolutely no way you can harm someone or control another person's free will with Reiki, it is still a bad idea to *wish* someone to do your will instead of her own.

DO NOT send, "I ask that my daughter go to MIT, become a rocket scientist and marry John Smith because I know that these things will make her life wonderful."
DO send, "I ask that my daughter be happy and successful in her career and in her relationships."

It is with some shame that I present the following story. The lessons I learned from the experience are important enough that I felt it must be shared.

When I first learned Reiki, another healer and I were emotionally involved with each other. This man introduced me to the use of crystals for healing. One of our favorite minerals was spodumene, a heart chakra stone. Whenever he asked me to send him healing, I sent it through a spodumene stone.

One evening we were at a class together when the whole fabric of our relationship suddenly changed. For hours we sat side by side, our arms just barely touching, surrounded by a glow that told even strangers that we were very much *together*. Later that evening, after a conversation with one of his friends, the energy suddenly shifted. He became extremely upset and then abruptly and completely closed himself off to me. It was as though he had become encased in a shroud of ice. I was heartbroken by the loss.

The next morning I pulled out the spodumene stone I always used to send him healing. In the past,

I had sent him healing with no more attachment to the outcome than to ask that the Reiki do what it needed to do. This time, without considering the implication of my actions, I attempted to reach out to him psychically through the stone that had once been a talisman to both of us. I attempted to reconstruct the energy lines between us. In essence, I tried to hold onto this man's spirit even though he no longer desired an association with me.

Two things happened. First, of course, the Reiki would not flow. Second, a few moments after I ended the session, the spodumene stone disappeared from my shirt pocket. I immediately understood the full implication of my actions. I had attempted to control another person's free will. The Reiki would not allow it. The stone left because I didn't deserve to carry it. I searched the area for days but never found that stone.

Understanding the lesson, I called and apologized to the man. I never again tried to bend another person's will with Reiki.

A second lesson was still to come from the incident. Almost eleven months to the day after the loss of my spodumene crystal (*the incidents were recorded in my journal*), the lesson arrived.

At that time I had been working with another healer for some weeks, trying to resolve some old traumas that still affected my present life. He led me back through multiple lifetimes, releasing traumas I had carried with me for millennia. The deeper we went, the more obvious it became that we were still far from the original source of the trauma that had resulted in a terrible, chronic pain in my right hip.

We believed my relationship with my mother throughout countless lifetimes was the origin of the trauma we were dealing with. He was afraid we might go through dozens more sessions and never get to the core of the issue. It was like following ripples in from the edges of a great lake and never finding the pebble that had set them in motion. We finally decided I needed to somehow use distance healing to resolve the situation.

During the drive home, I carefully chose the words and affirmations I would use to direct this distance healing. I knew I must send the healing in a way that would help me without causing any harm to my mother or to any other soul. I knew I must not ask for anything that could interfere with their free will.

By the time I arrived home, I had decided to simply send distance healing *to the event that was the origin of the Karma between my mother and myself.*

Before sending the distance healing, I walked out to my back porch and followed the path to the gazebo at the far end of the yard. Half-way down the path, I glanced down and saw a piece of broken glass lying at the side of the walkway, shining in the sunlight. I bent to pick up the glass shard so my dogs wouldn't step on it. What I picked up was not a piece of glass at all. It was the same spodumene crystal that had disappeared eleven months earlier when I attempted to misuse distance healing. Now that I had come to understand the cleanest, most powerful use of distance healing, I had become worthy of carrying the stone. So the stone returned to me.

Healing the Present

Buddhist philosophy teaches us to strive to live in the moment. The Reiki principles begin with the phrase, "Just for today..."

There is unquestionable value in healing the past to change the effect it has on our present lives. Healing the future may help us to attain goals and improve our lives. Still, one of the most important and powerful aspects of distance healing is healing the present.

Healing the present means using the added power of distance healing to go inside ourselves, to reach the very core of our being, and to ask to find peace and joy in who we are and in what we do.

In a time of loneliness and depression, I mourned for the spouse and family I had never had and began to resent the life I had chosen. My distance sessions became a time to ask, always to ask, for my life to change. The requests were carefully phrased so that I would not harm or remove the abundance from anyone else. There was nothing intrinsically wrong with any of the requests, and yet those sessions felt superficial and empty.

For a long time I couldn't understand why this was happening. I even began to feel that the healing wasn't working. Instead of experiencing the joy and elation I used to feel from performing a healing or caring for a patient, I began to harbor a mild resentment for the choices I had made. I longed for the life I might have had. The love and the joy were being replaced by anger and emptiness.

After a midnight session of misery and tears, I finally realized the anger and resentment were eating me alive, destroying the part of me that I loved best, the caretaker, the healer.

Turning off the light, I picked up the crystal I use as a focus for distance healing and began to send energy. Without any conscious effort on my part to search for the right words or the right requests, they all came out. I asked to be freed of the spirit of anger. I asked to be freed of the spirit of depression. I asked to be freed of the spirits of loneliness and discontent. I asked that the fragmented parts of my spirit be returned to me, to make me whole again. I asked to be filled with the spirit of love and joy that had been long gone. I asked to be once again filled with the joy I used to feel from being a vessel of healing for others. Instead of resenting the absence of various things from my life, and asking for things to go the way I thought they should, *I asked to be able to find joy and contentment in what I had.*

After setting down my paper, I fell into a deep, untroubled sleep. For the first time in months, I awoke the next morning feeling full, peaceful and content. Life was good again.

The scope of distance healing is limited only by your imagination. If you can think of a way to direct healing energy towards a goal or object *without causing harm or loss to anyone else*, it can be done.

Of course it was not I who cured,
It was the power from the outer world,
and visions and ceremonies had only made me like a hole
through which the power would come to the two-leggeds.
If I thought I was doing it by myself, the hole would close
up and no power would come through it.
~Black Elk Speaks
by Black Elk

CHAPTER TWENTY-FIVE

Integrating Healing Techniques

Over the years, I have attended every healing workshop I was able to fit into my schedule. They serve not only to increase my knowledge and skills but simply to help me understand what is possible. They also create a forum where a group of healers can come together to share their experiences and ideas, where we may experience the sheer joy of sharing healings.

I rarely perform a healing using one technique alone. Instead, I integrate all I have learned into each healing session. When I encounter an energy block during a healing, I invoke the Reiki Distance Symbol to direct the energy back to whatever past situation has caused the energy block. If that doesn't break through the block, I may attempt to scoop it away with my hands or to gather it into a crystal. If I still can't get through, then I may use other shamanic techniques or Brent Baum's system of holographic memory resolution. The methods all integrate beautifully.

Reflexology

The basic theory behind reflexology is that there are specific points on the foot that correspond to every part of the body. The same is true of the hand and the ear. The reflexologist treats her client by working on specific areas of the feet, hands or ears.

If a client is uneasy about being touched, a combination of guided imagery and ear reflexology will often help her to relax and allow her to become more receptive to the entire session. Someone who is unable to be touched because of a physical injury like a burn, or because of emotional pain resulting from a history of physical assault may only tolerate being touched on her hands, ears or feet. Since the ears or feet can reflex the entire body, an hour of Reiki flowing through those areas can be as effective as a full body treatment.

I have also discovered that running Reiki through one area of the body while using my other hand to direct Reiki energy through the corresponding hand or foot reflexology point can greatly intensify the effects of a treatment.

Using a sweeping movement, the practitioner's hands glide through the client's etheric energy field.

Therapeutic Touch

Therapeutic Touch is a form of energy work that was developed by nurses. The Therapeutic Touch practitioner works primarily in the etheric field, about four inches above her patient's body. Using a sweeping movement of her hands, beginning at the level of the patient's head and moving toward the feet, she smoothes out irregularities in her patient's energy field.

I often use Therapeutic Touch at the beginning of a healing session to help release energy blocks, and again at the end of the session to do a final clean up of the energy field.

If a client cannot tolerate any physical contact at all, the use of Reiki distance healing and Therapeutic Touch may be the only acceptable treatment modalities.

Dowsing

Dowsing is an ancient art. The implements of dowsing serve as a means of communication between the dowser and her spirit guides. The practitioner enlists the aide of willow rods, sticks, or pendulum to do everything from locating water in the earth to performing healings. Dowsing can be used to transmute harmful electromagnetic energy frequencies on a property into beneficial energies and to set a level of protection around the property. The dowsing system can be used to raise the love level in a house and to remove the spirits of depression, anger, and loneliness from a client.

Seeing these things done at a dowsing seminar, I realized that all these functions could be equally well accomplished using Reiki distance healing techniques. It had simply never occurred to me to do so. The methods are really very similar though, superficially, they appear quite different. Both techniques help the healer to focus and direct her intent and to enlist the aide of her spirit teachers and guides to perform healings.

Healing With Crystals

I have always been fascinated by crystals. I began to understand how they could be used for healing after a friend demonstrated how simply holding different minerals provided subtle mood alterations. I often use crystals as the focus of distance healing treatments. As previously discussed, crystals can also be extremely helpful in removing energy blocks.

It is important to cleanse crystals after any healing use. To do this, place them in a bath of sea salt and water for at least twenty-four hours. Upon removal, rinse them thoroughly under running water and then place them on a sunny window ledge to recharge. A number of other methods for cleaning crystals as well as a full encyclopedia of the metaphysical properties of different crystals can be found in Melody's book, *Love is in the Earth*.

Holographic Memory Resolution

Brent Baum has developed a system that uses a combination of talking and energy work to free a client of the effects of physical and emotional trauma. The client is guided back to the moment before the traumatic event occurred. She is then assisted in creating a mental image of an alternate outcome to the situation, one where the traumatic event did not occur. Finally, using color and sound, every cell of the client's body is cleared of the physical memory of the original trauma, and the client is healed.

Shamanic Healing

The winter of 1995-1996 was the most exciting period of my life. I was openly offering Reiki to all my labor and surgery patients and to anyone else who "wanted to see what it felt like." I was also going to weekly meetings at the Polarity Institute and meeting many other healers. Life was grand. I believed anything was possible.

During this period I attended a workshop taught by a man named Clinton Jarboe, a shaman from Canada. After the workshop, Clinton offered to teach me how to use energy to open up a woman's pelvis so it would be easier for her to give birth. We never did get around to the lesson, but apparently just being told it could be done was all the teaching that was required. In energy medicine, believing it is possible to do something can *make* it possible.

Some weeks after my session with Clinton, I was caring for an obstetrics patient who was trying to have a vaginal birth after a previous Caesarian section. Her first baby weighed seven pounds and eight ounces, and she had been sectioned because the baby was too big to fit through her pelvis.

As usual, I offered the woman a Reiki treatment when she was in labor. While working on her, I suddenly fell into a deep meditative state. It felt as though I was floating above the earth. Below, I saw my body, the body of a sleep walker, performing a healing on the woman. When my hands moved above her pelvis, they began to gently pull at the energy lines. I could *see* the bones arcing up, enlarging her pelvic outlet. Abruptly, I was back in my body, fully awake, completing the treatment. Within the hour, the woman easily delivered her ten pound one ounce son.

Shamanic Rituals

The essence of many shamanic rituals is to give physical form to an energetic problem and then, through the act of destroying the physical form, to relieve the problem. The physical image makes it easier for our conscious mind to comprehend and work with an energetic problem.

A simple example of this concept is a very basic shamanic technique for removing pain. The healer asks the client to describe her pain as if it were a physical object having a size, shape, texture, temperature, color and odor. Once the physical image is clearly established in the minds of both healer and client, the healer verbally describes the physical destruction of the image of the pain as she energetically removes it. This exercise makes the removal of the pain a real and physical event that the client, who may know nothing about energy work, is able to understand. It also allows the client, through her visualization, to participate in her own healing process. Taking part in her own healing empowers the client and intensifies the healing.

What is healing after all if it is not regaining power over one's own existence?

Karmic Core Cleansing

I was first exposed to one of my favorite shamanic healing techniques at Clinton's workshop. He calls this technique karmic core cleansing.

The karmic core is an energy region in the client's etheric field above her spine. It originates at the level of the crown chakra and goes all the way to the first chakra. It is a location where stress, negative emotions, and the trauma of negative experiences are often stored. This technique helps the healer to remove the stored negative energy.

This procedure is generally saved for the end of a healing session. Prior to beginning, the healer should shield herself and visualize her hands in protective silver gloves. She will be handling a lot of negative energy and does not want to pick up any of it herself.

The client is asked to lie on her stomach on a massage table or other flat surface. The healer uses her hands to read the energy field about four inches above the client's spine. She is trying to detect the presence of stores of dense, negative energy in that area.

The healer picks up a crystal scalpel. (*I generally choose black kyanite though I have seen quartz crystals used equally well.*) She uses the crystal and her intent to make an incision into the client's energy field. The incision begins above the crown chakra and moves down the length of the spine to about four inches below the junction of the legs at the end of the first chakra. Two other incisions are made above the path of the sciatic nerves which begin at the level of the sacrum and travel through the buttocks and down the top third of the thigh. (*see illustration*). The healer should visualize these areas opening as she makes her incision. It is her mind and intent that direct the physical process. The crystal is merely a vehicle for focusing her intent.

Once the area has been opened, the healer picks up a crystal sphere or egg. Any mineral that will remove energy blocks and collect negative energy can be used. (*I generally prefer either smoky or rose quartz. On occasion I have used labradorite, calcite, and black onyx for this purpose.*)

Standing at the left side of her client, the healer holds the sphere in her left hand. Beginning at the level of the crown chakra, the healer slowly rolls the sphere down the length of her client's spine. At the same time she uses her right hand to gather together the negative energy from the karmic core and guide it into the sphere. The motion resembles one that might be used to gather cake crumbs from the top of a table. It usually takes several minutes to complete this process. After clearing down to the first chakra, she moves the crystal back to the sacral area. Using the same collection technique, the negative energy is swept from the left and then the right sciatic areas. When the collection is finished, the crystal should immediately be dropped into a container that has been filled with water and sea salt and left to soak for twenty-four hours. The crystal, now filled with negative energy, should be handled as little as possible.

My students and I have observed two changes within the crystal spheres when this technique is performed. As the spheres collect the energy being cleaned away, they often become cloudy and may exhibit a color change. They also become much heavier to hold.

After the stone has been placed in the salt water, the healer returns to her client. First, she smoothes the energy field above her client's spine. She may then grasp the top and bottom ends of the client's karmic core in her hands at the same time and tug on them gently to smooth everything out. This is the ultimate chiropractic adjustment since it smoothes out the energy core that the spine reflects. She then uses her hands and her intent to re-seal the case of the karmic core. Then she once again smoothes the surface. It is important to leave the surface even and level to allow optimal flow of energy.

Similar techniques are used in many shamanic cultures. The Kahunas of Hawaii use an egg instead of a crystal to collect the negative energy. When they are done, they boil the egg to trap the negative energy. Some native healers sweep with an eagle feather and manually clear the negative energy away.

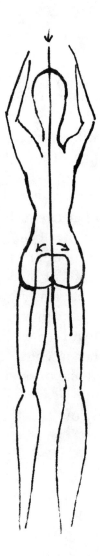

karmic core cleansing

People usually feel lighter after a karmic core cleansing. Alice came up to me the next day and said, "I feel as though I have been exorcised."

Mark, who was going through a difficult period of his life, came to my house for a healing session. He arrived brimming with stress and anxiety. It actually took an hour and a half of Reiki before the worry lines in his forehead disappeared and his face relaxed. (*Usually this happens in the first few minutes of a session.*) At that point, we went outside to play with my horses for a while. When we came back in, I worked on him again. At the end of the second session, I performed a karmic core cleansing using my favorite smoky quartz sphere to remove the negative energy that had been stored above his spine. At the end of the treatment, as always, I placed the crystal sphere into a bath of salt water to neutralize the negative energy. Twenty-four hours later, I placed the sphere in a flower bed in the sunshine to recharge. The crystal shattered.

The next day, Mark called me on the phone and said, "You know, I don't really believe in that crystal stuff, I just let you do it to be polite, but now I'm beginning to think there's something to it. Yesterday, at work, a client said some things that would normally send me off into a screaming rage, but this time the situation didn't even phase me. I guess what you did to remove the anger I was carrying must have worked." I never told him about the shattered crystal.

Shamanic Journeys

Another basic tool of the shamanic healer is the shamanic journey. The healer uses various techniques to shift into an altered state of consciousness, a state that is in many ways, similar to a deep meditative state. In this state, she journeys outside the boundaries of ordinary reality to times and places where she can obtain information that is pertinent to a healing.

In the fall of 1996, I had the privilege of attending a workshop on Celtic Shamanism taught by Tom Cowan. Tom's workshop and his book, *Fire in the Head*, finally brought me in touch with all the ancient Celtic myths and spiritual concepts that I was searching for, but had not found, on my trip to Findhorn, Scotland.

It wasn't until I attended Tom's workshop that I realized just how much of what I had been drawn to in the fantasy books I loved so much was based on genuine Celtic history and tradition and not just the author's imagination.

For me, the high point of this workshop came when Tom led us on a shamanic journey that turned us all into poets. First, Tom explained Tuirgin. The Gaelic word describes the Celtic belief that one can be reincarnated not only as a person but as an animal, a plant, a season. The Celts say that one may spend an entire lifetime as the wind in the trees. Then, with his drum and his voice, he guided us on a journey through time and space. He encouraged us to revisit lifetimes spent as plant and beast, as place and season. Before beginning, we were instructed to sit up and write our experiences in our notebooks as soon as we returned from the journey.

When I began to write, the words flowed from my pen of their own accord as images flew through my mind. After a moment or two, it was over. I lay down my pen and read what I had just written. Scribbled in my journal were the following words:

I am cool summer rain
I am the interminable heat of the desert summer sun
I am the tree of life, my roots anchored deep in the rocky places of the earth,
my branches glistening in sunlight trembling in the wind
I am time immortal
I am the watching one, the grandfather
I am the deer, still, watchful, waiting
I am the deer, mother of the earth
I am the deer, guardian of stillness
I am the desert hiding the gift of life
I am the desert with spiny edges and hidden beauties
I am the desert eternal
I am the goddess, nurturing and healing
I am the one who shapes thoughts for the mind

Recommended Reading

Empowerment Through Reiki, Paula Horan, Lotus Light-Shangrila Press 1996

Essential Reiki, Diane Stein, The Crossing Press 1996

Soul Retrieval, Sandra Ingerman, HarperSanFrancisco 1991

Fire in the Head, Tom Cowan, HarperSanFrancisco,1993

Love is in the Earth, Melody, Earth-Love Publishing House 1995

Anatomy of the Spirit, Caroline Myss, Three Rivers Press 1996

Healing Ceremonies, Howard Silverman, M.D.and Carl A. Hammerschlag, M.D., Perigree Health 1997

Conversations With God, Neale Donald Walsch, G.P. Putnam's Sons 1995

Reiki: a Torch in Daylight, Karyn Mitchell, Ph.D., Mind Rivers Publications 1994

Creative Visualizations, Shakti Gawain,Bantam Starfire 1983

A Letter to Robin, Walt Woods, The American Society of Dowsers 1998

Healing Resolution, Brent Baum, www.healingresolution.com

Working With Your Chakras, Ruth White, Samuel Weiser Inc. 1994

About the Author

Jeri Mills lives in the desert outside of Tucson, Arizona. She shares her home with three dogs, two cats, two horses and a miniature donkey. She continues to study, to teach and to write. She still listens to the sahuaros.

Dr. Mills opened her own medical practice, Green Valley Women's Health Care, in 1997. Her patients are as likely to receive a Reiki treatment or a recipe as they are a prescription.

Dr. Mills received her first doctorate, in veterinary medicine, from Ohio State University in May of 1980. After practicing veterinary medicine for three years, she attended medical school and earned an M.D. degree in 1987. She spent the next four years completing a residency program in Obstetrics and Gynecology at The State University of New York at Buffalo. After working for two years in Kingsport, Tennessee, she relocated to Tucson Arizona. She has been a Reiki Master Teacher since 1995.

Visit us on the WEB at
www.TapestryOfHealing.Com